Saving Our Cities

You Can Change Your City for God

by
Happy Caldwell

Harrison House
Tulsa, Oklahoma

Unless otherwise indicated, all Scripture quotations are taken from the *King James Version* of the Bible.

Scripture quotations marked AMP are taken from *The Amplified Bible, Old Testament*. Copyright © 1965, 1987 by the Zondervan Corporation, Grand Rapids, Michigan. Used by permission.

Contents

Introduction

God wants to be the God of every city in the world! Think for a moment about the cities in the various nations of the earth. *Jerusalem* means "City of Peace." Christopher Columbus named the first place he set foot in Central America *San Salvador*, which means "City of our Holy Savior." Then think for a moment what God intended for the nation of England, as it is stately named, "The United Kingdom," or America, which is called "The United States." It is time for us, as the body of Christ, to grasp and fulfill the vision God intends for the cities and nations of the earth!

We have many examples here in America: *Los Angeles* means "The City of Angels"; *Corpus Christi*, "The Body of Christ"; *Salem*, "Peace." If you will take the time to research the history of your city, you may find somewhere along the line that God had a part in the founding of it.

There is an interesting theme that runs throughout the Word of God — *God is a God of cities*, and He has a specific order for us to follow in preaching the gospel to our cities. For instance, in the book of Acts, we can read the last commission Jesus gave the disciples before the Holy Spirit descended:

> But ye shall receive power, after that the Holy Ghost is come upon you: and ye shall be witnesses unto me both in Jerusalem, and in all Judaea, and in Samaria, and unto the uttermost part of the earth.
>
> Acts 1:8

Many times when we read that verse, we only focus on the first half of the paragraph. Some of us get so caught up

5

in the power of God that we forget what to do with it. It *is* important that we receive the power of the Holy Spirit, but notice the reason: *to be witnesses in our city* (Jerusalem); *state or province* (Judaea); *nation* (Samaria); *and elsewhere in the world!*

All through the New Testament, we are exhorted to heed the words of Jesus and to keep them in the midst of our hearts and minds. In Acts 1:8, we see a precedent Jesus has set for us to follow in ministering the power of the Holy Spirit to the people of the earth: first to the city, then the state or province, then the nation and elsewhere in the earth.

We see that God cares about the nations, but what makes up a nation? What makes up a state or province? It's not the scenery. It's not the industry or the wildlife. It's the *cities!*

The term "city" does not refer to buildings and utilities and transportation. The term "city" is defined as an *"organized population center."* When you look at your city, it does not just consist of the skyscrapers, the post office, or the general store. *People make up your city.* Just like the church is not a building but a group of *people*, your city is the *people*. Remember this: God is a God of people and people make up cities. There are no cities without people, only empty blocks of cement and asphalt.

Many have endeavored to reach a city. However, after the newness, the excitement, and the momentum were gone, so was the commitment. For this reason, probably the most important chapters, and at the same time the least exciting, are the ones that deal with character, diligence, integrity, and commitment. The roots of character are what hold a spiritual tree in the ground as it grows. Without character, there will never be any lasting work to reach your city.

In 1979, when God told us to build a church in Little Rock, specifically a spiritual production center, He not only told us, "I will deliver the city into your hands for the preaching of the gospel," but He also told me I was not the first preacher He had called to do what He wanted done. He told me I was the seventh.

That is pretty humbling when you know you were not God's first choice! I asked Him who the others were and why they failed. He not only showed me who they were, but He showed me where each church had made its mistake so I would not make the same ones.

I don't pretend to suggest others have not made a difference in their cities. They have. I also am not suggesting that we have a *Christian* city or a perfect city. We don't yet. However, I know the principles and formulas I am sharing in this book have worked in our city.

I have waited several years before writing this book. I wanted to *prove* that *God is a God of cities* before I wrote about it, because God tells us to prove Him (Malachi 3:10). He does not worry; He cannot lie; and if we trust Him, apply His Word, and don't get weary in well doing, we shall reap.

It takes hard work and diligence to accomplish a vision. It takes honesty and integrity to stay humble and small in your own eyes. You must always remind yourself that it is not you, but God working through you, that has wrought the victory.

You are strategically placed in your city for a purpose. You are there because God created you and He has something for you to do. He has placed your church there for a reason and a purpose. He has placed your pastor there for a reason and a purpose. That purpose is to advance the kingdom of God according to His plan for your city.

Not only do I have a vision for my city, but I also believe I have found a scripture about "Little Rock" in the Bible! In Matthew 16:18 Jesus said to Peter, **Thou art Peter** [rock],

and upon this [little rock] I will build my church; and the gates of hell shall not prevail against it. Well, in the records at the court house in Little Rock, Arkansas, it is recorded that the city name is "Little Rock," and the township in which it is located is called "Big Rock." How about that!

I don't believe it was a coincidence that I was born in Little Rock, Arkansas. I love our city. Many times when my wife and I fly in and out of Little Rock, we are blessed when we see the skyline, the office buildings, and the homes that the people occupy. Something happens in our hearts when we look at our city. God has given us this city in the Spirit. Little Rock, Arkansas, is on the inside of us, in our hearts. Even though we don't know all the people living here, we have laid down our lives for them.

There are approximately half a million people in the metroplex where we minister. These people have the same choice as any other populated city — they must decide if Jesus is to be their Lord or not. My wife, myself, and our church have been placed by God to be a visible pathway for them. We believe with all our hearts that "Jesus is Lord over Little Rock...and your city too!"

Chapter 1
Eden — A City of Beginnings

Although men build cities today, God built the first city. In Genesis 2:8, we read: **And the Lord God planted a garden eastward in Eden; and there he put the man whom he had formed.**

Most of the time when we read this scripture, we only think of the *garden* of Eden, but God says He *planted a garden eastward* in Eden.

The city of Eden was real and God built it. The name *Eden* means, "City of Beginnings" or "City of Peace." The city of Eden was planned by God to be a city of peace, delight, and pleasantness. Eden was a beginning. Then, God planted a garden east in that city and placed the man whom He had formed in it. You might say Adam was the first suburbanite!

Archaeologists discovered and excavated a city which the Babylonians called "Eridu." The name of this city translated in English is "Eden." When the British excavated Eden in 1918, the statement they included in their findings was that the city was extremely prosperous. Ancient writings say, "Near Eridu [Eden] was a garden, in which was a mysterious sacred tree, a tree of life, planted by God, whose roots were deep, while its branches reached to heaven, protected by guardian spirits, and no man enters." (See *Halley's Bible Handbook*, Archaeological Note: Eridu, Traditional Garden of Eden, pp. 65,66.)

If we read further in Genesis 2, we find that a river flowed out from the city of Eden to water the Garden; and from the Garden it divided into four heads. The geology surrounding these four rivers was of very high quality: gold, pearl and onyx (Genesis 2:10-14). Located on the Persian Gulf, Eden was the house of man, animals, and most of our fruits and vegetables. Eden was the cradle of civilization.

If we had lived in Eden during the time of Adam, there would never have been a need to leave the city. Although the mind and heart of God never changed concerning the destiny of Eden, we all know what happened to the city. God intended for us to inherit Eden, to dwell in a city of peace, surrounded by riches and wealth. He intended for us to eat from and enjoy the luscious vegetation in the Garden He planted eastward of the city. He intended for us to populate and begin other cities so the earth could be inhabited and prospered by God's people. (Genesis 1:28,29.)

For example, Cain built the first man-made city. Genesis 4:17 says, **And he builded a city, and called the name of the city, after the name of his son, Enoch.** That was the plan of God. God had built the first city and He told Adam and Eve to take care of it. They were to populate that city and send their offspring out to begin other cities, populate them, and rule over them for God.

Had Adam and Eve kept the dominion God had delivered into their hands, there would have never been any sin on the earth. There would have never been a heathen. There would never have been any evil or any enemies of God. Every city that would have been established by the offspring of Adam and Eve would have been a godly city, and God would have been Lord over it.

What caused the decay and corruption of Eden, the oldest city in the Bible? The spirit of rebellion. As we read Ezekiel 28:11-15, we see that Lucifer had his reign over that city before Adam was created.

Moreover the word of the Lord came unto me, saying, Son of man, take up a lamentation upon the king of Tyrus, and say unto him, Thus saith the Lord God; Thou sealest up the sum, full of wisdom, and perfect in beauty. Thou hast been in Eden the garden of God; every precious stone was thy covering, the sardius, topaz, and the diamond, the beryl, the onyx, and the jasper, the sapphire, the emerald, and the carbuncle, and gold: the workmanship of thy tabrets and of thy pipes was prepared in thee in the day that thou wast created. Thou art the anointed cherub that covereth; and I have set thee so: thou wast upon the holy mountain of God; thou hast walked up and down in the midst of the stones of fire. Thou wast perfect in thy ways from the day that thou wast created, till iniquity was found in thee.

In the next part of this Scripture, we find the key that caused the corruption of Eden through the influence of Lucifer:

By the multitude of thy merchandise (possessions, subjects) they have filled the midst of thee with violence, and thou hast sinned: therefore I will cast thee as profane out of the mountain of God: and I will destroy thee, O covering cherub, from the midst of the stones of fire. Thine heart was lifted up because of thy beauty, thou hast corrupted thy wisdom by reason of thy brightness: I will cast thee to the ground, I will lay thee before kings, that they may behold thee. Thou hast defiled thy sanctuaries by the multitude of thine iniquities, by the iniquity of thy traffick....

Ezekial 28:16-18

What did God mean, *iniquity of traffick*? *Traffick* means "trade." In the city of Eden, there was commerce and business, just as you and I know it. Due to the tremendous wealth of the city, there was buying and selling, organization and government. The city operated under God's law and order. We tend to think that government, business, trade, and the gross national product are provisions from our generation alone. No, it all operated from the very beginning. Heaven is the most organized and efficient place in the universe because it is run by God. He patterned the city of Eden after Heaven, just as we were patterned after God.

God had a plan for Eden. Lucifer had been sent to this city and to the Garden to provide supervision, but he became a corrupt politician. He became corrupted by the trade and traffic that transpired in that city. Because there was such order, beauty, and wealth, the subjects of the city began to praise and worship Lucifer because of his leadership. All of a sudden he began to think, "I will be like the Most High."

> **For thou hast said in thine heart, I will ascend into heaven, I will exalt my throne above the stars of God: I will sit also upon the mount of the congregation, in the sides of the north: I will ascend above the heights of the clouds; I will be like the most High.**
> **Isaiah 14:13,14**

God does not tolerate anarchy. He doesn't hold a board meeting or take a popular vote on what action to take when a spirit of rebellion surfaces. His verdict is based on His righteousness.

> **Yet thou shall be brought down to hell, to the sides of the pit. They that see thee shall narrowly look upon thee, and consider thee, saying, Is this the man that made the earth to tremble, that did shake kingdoms; That made the world as a wilderness, and destroyed the cities thereof.**
> **Isaiah 14:15-17**

Why does a city become evil? Because of the people. Why do the people become evil? Why do the people create an evil city? It is because they worship an evil god. *For every crippled or destroyed city there is a principality, a power, a ruler of darkness and millions of wicked spirits that are sent out to attack that city.* (See Daniel 10:13.)

You may say, "Well, can't God do anything to stop it?" If the people of a city reject God and continually live in sin, God will take His people out of the city and let it destroy itself by the sin it produced. God will never go *against* your will to *change* your will, but He will raise up intercessors to stand in the gap for the people of the city. He will answer their righteous petitions. Abraham stood up and did business for God at Sodom and Gomorrah. He said, **Wilt thou also destroy the righteous with the wicked?** (Genesis 18:23).

It's the intercessors and the men and women God raises up to proclaim the gospel who change the course of cities and nations, not the politicians. I have found an exciting pattern throughout the Bible in which men were identified with their cities: Jesus of Nazareth; Saul of Tarsus; Jerusalem, City of David.

Twelve miles north of Eden was the City of Ur, the home of Abraham. I have seen the excavation of Ur in the British Museum in London. It, too, was a highly prosperous and industrious city with underground sewer systems and libraries.

Seventy miles north of Eden was Fara, the City of Noah. Noah was one of those righteous men who was called to reach his city for God. [God] **spared not the old world, but saved Noah the eighth person, a preacher of righteousness** (2 Peter 2:5).

The word *person* is italicized in the Bible, which means it was added for clarity by the translators. However, Noah was not the eighth "person" from Adam. If you read the genealogies in Genesis 5, you will note "unnamed" sons and daughters. There were innumerable children born that were not named to us. Only the men who were to preach righteousness to their cities were named — and numbered — which means God is establishing a pattern.

If you read the verse correctly and without the word *person,* the writer is saying, "God saved Noah, the eighth preacher of righteousness." Let's establish this in the mouth of two or three witnesses. In the book of Jude, verse fourteen, the writer says, **And Enoch also, the seventh from Adam....** Again, by checking the genealogy in Genesis 5, we know Enoch was not the seventh "person" because of the unnamed sons and daughters. Therefore he had to be the seventh preacher of righteousness. (Read Genesis 5 and Hebrews 11.)

Here we see God's pattern and purpose: To place righteous men in cities to proclaim Him as God over those cities. In our day, that pattern continues. When you think of Tulsa, Oklahoma, you think of Oral Roberts and Kenneth Hagin; Minneapolis, Minnesota, Billy Graham; Fort Worth, Texas, Kenneth Copeland, and so on.

Chapter 2
The Spiritual Prerequisite

In Paul's first letter to the Corinthians, he could not expound the wisdom that was intended because the people were carnal. He said, **And I, brethren, could not speak unto you as unto spiritual, but as unto carnal, even as unto babes in Christ** (1 Corinthians 3:1).

You may wonder what that scripture has to do with reaching your city for God. Paul is writing here that he could not teach those people spiritual principles because they were carnal. To be carnal means to remain in our human nature. God never intended for us to remain in our human, carnal nature. He intended for us to be spiritual. The whole reason Paul wanted to talk to them about spiritual things is because they were supposed to go out into the harvest and win their city, Corinth, to the Lord.

We are here to bring in the harvest for God. That is our whole purpose. Why do we build churches? Why do we build mission schools, Christian schools, television stations, and so on? It is for the sole reason of bringing in the harvest of people and turning them to Jesus Christ.

Carnal Character

Carnality is an enemy in reaching a city for God. The wisdom and revelation from God cannot flow through a carnal person because they are spiritual babes. A spiritual babe is **unskilful in the word of righteousness** (Hebrews 5:13). They do not know who they are in Christ, nor can they discern good from evil. Spiritual babes must be fed the "easy" principles of God, for they do not allow themselves to be groomed by the whole Word of God. They "pick and choose" what they want to hear because they are full of envying, strife, and divisions. This nature of man is quickly angered and easily offended. Carnal people refuse to take responsibility for their Christian walk. They are unsteady, unreliable, and talkative. The carnal man makes quick commitments but never finishes the course. No person can reach a city and win it to God with that kind of character. Instead, the city will turn on them and make them a laughing spectacle in the end.

Spiritual Character

Before we can adequately reach our cities for God, there are spiritual principles that must be cultivated in our lives. Being "spiritual" does not mean walking around with our heads so far in the clouds that we are no earthly good. It doesn't mean we are "super saints" or that we are better than anyone else. Being spiritual doesn't mean we have a prophetic word for everyone we meet.

We are recreated beings the minute we become born again, but we must harness and groom our human nature and season it with the Word of God in order to walk spiritually. Spiritual growth begins in the root of our character. It has nothing to do with a "vapor" or a "mist" or a "far away look" in our eyes. Instead, it is a "pull up your boot straps and roll up your sleeves" day-to-day walk with God. As we fellowship daily with the Lord and continue in the Word of God, we become spiritual.

There are imperative keys in reaching our cities for God, and they are in the realm of spiritual character. We can never succeed in doing anything for Christ if we are in it for ourselves, or act as the carnal, unregenerate man.

Your spiritual gift *alone* cannot reach a city for God. For centuries some men and women have relied on their spiritual gift alone to open doors and build ministries. Those ministries don't last long. Inner character is what "builds the house." A spiritual gift is simply that — a "gift" from God. That gift is to adorn and compliment the inner character a person continues to build through the years by the Word of God and the guidance of the Holy Spirit.

The character of Christ within a person is the "pillar" that holds and lifts up Jesus through that gift. We can never fall prey to the fabrication that being a great orator or a popular singer is enough to carry us. Popularity alone doesn't reach a city for God or keep His harvest growing and bearing fruit. *God requires His men and women to be spiritual in character.* It is hard work to reach a city and bring in the harvest, and we are in the season of the greatest harvest the earth has ever seen! It is time to make ourselves the spiritual people God called us to be.

Chapter 3
Reaching Your City With Character

The Bible says in John 3:16, **For God so loved the world, that he gave his only begotten Son, that whosoever believeth in him should not perish, but have everlasting life.**

When Jesus brought the gospel into the earth, it cost Him something. To His people to operate in the power of the gospel (the promises of the Bible), it will cost them something as well.

We are the "whosoevers" through whom God desires to bring the power of the gospel into the world. If we believe Jesus, then this entire *world* belongs to *us* for the preaching of the gospel! However, as believers, in order to affect and win our cities, we must be willing to lay down our human nature and put on the **character** of Christ.

Character Is Measured

For I say, through the grace given unto me, to every man that is among you, not to think of himself more highly than he ought to think; but to think soberly, according as God hath dealt to every man the measure of faith.

Romans 12:3

After reading that verse, you may be thinking, "I don't see anything about 'character' being measured in a person. All I see is that 'faith' is measured." But this verse is telling us that faith and character are dependent upon one another. The measure of faith is used as we appropriate God's grace not to think of ourselves more highly than we ought — which is character.

Your faith is the result, the demonstration, and the productivity of your character. For example, if you are out of God's will, in sin, or in disobedience (which is a lack of character), you will have little faith to believe for anything. Why is this so? When your character is wrong, you are out of fellowship with God. Being out of fellowship with God, you are obviously not having any faith in Him or His Word! So you can see how your character affects your level of faith.

On the other hand, the level of character in a person depends on their level of faith. Without any faith, we cannot demonstrate any character. It is our faith in God which gives us the strength to have character. For example, faith in God's promises gives us the courage to give sacrificially when He asks us, to lay hands on a sick person who is contagious, or to tell a neighbor about our relationship with Jesus. Our faith is the fuel for the demonstration of character in our lives.

Faith fuels character and character is the foundation for faith. They work together. Because the Bible says that faith is measured, character must also be measured.

Faith and Character

When we think of character, we usually think of honesty, goodness, faithfulness, and truth. When we sum it all up, we *are* what our character portrays. Everything we *do*, everything we *speak*, every way we *live* shows our character. We cannot show our faith without our character being seen, because we show our faith to others by our *works*. (James 2:14-26.)

In Hebrews 10:38, the Bible says, **The just** (the righteous, the redeemed — those who have character) **shall live by faith.** Faith in what? The Word of God. Our faith is demonstrated by our acts of character. If a person came to me and said he was "of great character," I would be looking for his level of faith and the way he demonstrated it. In other words, I would be looking at his lifestyle.

Your city will be looking at your lifestyle to determine whether or not you have character as well as faith. They know it is easy to say you have faith in God, but until they see your faith demonstrate character in your lifestyle, they will not take your witness seriously.

Furthermore, there are different types of faith. There is the God-kind of faith and there is natural faith. There are people in the world who don't know God and are not Christians; yet they have natural faith in the things they do. They are successful in the world because they have faith in themselves and their own abilities.

But natural faith crumbles when energy is depleted. Natural faith won't keep your family from generational curses. Natural faith is not multifaceted; it can only focus well on one particular area. It doesn't have the capacity to keep a mind from sin and depression, keep a marriage intact, and operate a multi-billion dollar industry at the same time. Natural faith can "burn out" and become exhausted because it depends on the person's frame of mind. A successful business can be lost when the person with natural faith dies.

To reach a city with the gospel, we must also have the God-kind of faith. We have all been given the measure of faith. (Romans 12:3.) If a person shows more results from his faith than others, it is because he used or exercised his faith to get to that level. That person did something with their measure.

Character is the same. We have all been given a measure of character when we were born again, but we must use and exercise that character in day-to-day situations to be

21

established by it. If someone appears to have greater character, it is because the person groomed themselves by the Word of God in everyday circumstances.

Character and Anointing

Just as faith and character work together, so do character and the anointing. There is a powerful anointing on a Christian who walks in the character of Christ, or God's Word, on a day-to-day basis. On the other hand, it is impossible to walk in the character of Christ without appropriating the anointing of the Holy Spirit throughout the day.

In simple terms, character and anointing happen together when we walk according to God's Word and in continuous intimacy with the Holy Spirit.

The anointing I'm talking about here is not the anointing on a ministry gift, but the day-to-day anointing any child of God can walk in. The anointing on a pulpit minister or ministry gift works differently, because the minister is a vessel through which God blesses His people. The minister is giving out; he is usually not receiving anything.

Because the minister is not placing himself in a position to receive for himself, but for others, he doesn't usually get any personal healing, instruction, or correction from the Holy Spirit. The only character-building aspect of the ministry gift anointing is when a minister maintains their awe and humility at being used by God in this powerful way, or when they actually apply instruction given to others to their own life.

This is why many ministers and congregation members mistake character for the anointing. When a minister is operating in their gift, that is the closest to perfection they will ever get while on earth, because the anointing is *God*, not the person. Thus, they can appear to be a perfect human being. This is because the anointing is very convincing and appealing.

The purpose of the anointing is to draw people to God.

Few understand what the anointing actually is. That is why so many people place ministers on a "pedestal." They only see them when they are operating under their ministry-gift anointing. They don't realize ministers are human beings with real problems to solve just like them.

The greater problem comes when the *minister* begins to focus on their gift more than their character. Too many ministries have fallen because the character of the person was not sufficiently groomed to match the gift. A great ministry gift can have a tremendous impact if great character is behind it. If character is not groomed with the gift, the ministry will have just a fraction of the impact it could have had.

Noah, Abraham, Moses, David, and Paul all operated under the anointing of God, but they were also men of character. Although God never recalls a ministry gift (Romans 11:29), some fold up completely due to lack of character. Those ministers destroyed themselves and their ministries, because they never heeded God's intention for their character to match their anointing.

How do you find a person's character — by how anointed they are as a minister? No. You find a person's character by watching their daily lifestyle of faith. What they *do* speaks louder than what they say.

What does the pastor *do* when times get hard? What does the ladies' Bible teacher *do* when symptoms try to attach themselves to her body? What does the Sunday school teacher do when someone speaks evil of them?

What does the deacon *do* when poverty comes? What does the youth pastor *do* when crisis or hardship come?

What does the children's church secretary *do* if temptation comes? Whatever is being developed inside them is going to come out.

The Bible says we have the mind of Christ, so His character is also ours. But how do we develop His character? Again, we go back to the simple basics of the Christian faith: Abide in God's Word and stay intimate with the Holy Spirit at all times and in all circumstances.

When ministers come down from their pulpit and line their everyday lives up with God's Word, constantly seeking the fellowship of the Holy Spirit during the day, they will develop character along with their ministry gift. They will have an anointing on their day-to-day lives, not just their ministry.

This is a powerful example to both their congregation and their city. Then, when their congregation follows after them in an anointed lifestyle of faith and character, their city will be flooded with Christians who are drawing every man, woman, and child they meet to Jesus Christ!

Demonstration of Character

Character is vital in reaching a city for God. Whether you are seen or unseen by the masses, you will be a witness to someone. There are many people in our church whose calling, instruction, or anointing from the Lord will not be seen by the multitudes. Yet God has given them individual missions because He knows their character represents the vision of reaching our city. God entrusts them with an assignment because He knows, although they might not be publicly seen, they will accomplish their task and therefore be a vital blessing to our city.

For example, one year at Christmas, God instructed me to have our church financially bless the Little Rock Police Department. We did so according to 1 Timothy 2:2 and Romans 13, respecting the authority in our city. Dedicated to reaching their city for God, our people prepared themselves and many gave a double tithe, sowing into the city of Little Rock. Not only did they bring double their tithes, they brought sacks of groceries for the poor, and our children brought new toys for the needy children.

The altar in our great auditorium was filled from one side to the other as our people raised their hands to heaven and worshipped God, thanking Him for our city. Needless to say, the Police Department was overwhelmed. We received countless letters showing their gratitude, and some of the families said they would not have made it that year if we had not given.

The city was startled that a people could love them and care for them without even knowing them, especially since their particular line of work goes so often without gratitude. *That selfless act of love toward the authority of our city turned their eyes toward God.*

The Chief of Police came in tears that year to our Christmas banquet and received a plaque showing our thankfulness, along with our check for $10,000. Several of the officers came dressed in their uniforms to our church. They were invited guests at another Christmas banquet, and our people preferred them first in line as we fed their families.

Although that particular incident was years ago, they still continually patrol our church grounds, watching over our property! To this day, a representative of the Police Department shows up with a special appreciation of some sort when we have a special function.

My point is this: Although the Police Department never knew what church member gave what, the people knew that God saw what they did. They were *individually* obedient to do what God had required of us; and since they *individually* participated as a *whole* body, God was able to bless our city through them.

Many of our people demonstrated their character by giving *double* their tithes in a holiday season when most would hold onto every penny they could. These people, through their growing character, sacrificed to do without at Christmas so *God* could be seen in their city.

We don't have to be seen by many to have great results. We don't have to be seen by many to have great character. All we need to do is have faith in God and obey Him.

Growing in Character

Character may begin in small ways. If we exercise our character, it will grow to be the most distinguishable attribute we have. Just as a weight-lifter exercises his muscles to make them larger and stronger, we must exercise our character in order for it to become stronger in our lives.

The Bible says in Matthew 13:31,32 that although the mustard seed is the tiniest of seeds, it is the greatest among herbs when it is full grown, and the branches of the mustard tree are so strong that the birds find secure lodging there. The chapter continues in verse 33, saying the kingdom of Heaven is likened to leaven, and that small leaven placed in 7.5 gallons of meal eventually leavens the whole lot.

Character begins the same way. Although it may start small in our lives, it will grow to become the anchor of our reputation. When we take the measure of character given to us and use it, it will grow.

How much is the measure of character we have received? It is enough to start and finish the course set before us. The point is, what are we doing with the measure of character we have? It is imperative to practice our character in day-to-day situations so when the emergencies come, when the large projects come, we can handle them in the character of Christ.

Years ago, the Lord told me that if I could build a church debt-free and keep the people from strife and church-splits, then I would be ready for the next project. Now I understand why. For ten years, God was grooming my character for the next phase of ministry. If I successfully passed the first ten years under the prerequisites He set forth, then I could "graduate" to the next undertaking.

There is no way we could have built our first television station in 1988 and begin broadcasting Channel 25, Arkansas' first full-power 24-hour Christian television station, without having gone through the first ten years of trials, emergencies, problems, and blessings. Those first ten years developed and established character in our ministry and church body.

Operating a television network that broadcasts throughout a large part of the state presents all sorts of challenges. Had we not developed the character necessary for this task during the first stage of our ministry, these challenges could have destroyed us and the people involved. All the oppositions, the regulations, the hurdles, the finances, the doubt, and the politics we were up against could have thoroughly defeated us. The city and state would have made us a laughingstock. Instead, they are having to look toward God, for obviously He is doing His work in our city.

Our people see Victory Television Network as a "window of heaven" from which flows deliverance, healing, and salvation to the people of our city and state. When a ministry is on television 24-hours a day, they had better be able to exemplify the character of Christ to the best of their ability.

The people of a city will evaluate your character by what they have seen you speak and do. Character accepts responsibility. We must be willing to take the responsibility ourselves to increase the measure of faith and character in our lives. The members of the body of Christ who obtain the revelation and responsibility of character in their lives will be the ones who lead in bringing in this great harvest. They won't be proud or lofty in their leading — they will have character.

The Measuring Stick of Character

In reaching a city, character should be our number one goal. To measure your character, put up a "spiritual ruler" in your mind and mark where you are in your growth according to the Word of God.

Dr. Lester Sumrall made a statement in our church concerning tithes and offerings. He said, "Men count what you give. God counts what you hold back." Take that same principle and apply it to character. Men pat you on the back for what you have accomplished. God requires us to answer for what we failed to accomplish due to a lack of character. We can only fail if we willfully choose not to correct the areas in our lives where character is lacking.

Luke, chapter 6, gives us good insight in marking the roots of character in our lives. In reaching a city for God, especially if we are in leadership, these verses are a good ruler in character and faith measurement.

> **But I say unto you which hear, Love your enemies, do good to them which hate you.**
> **Luke 6:27**

In reaching our cities for God, we will come against numerous uprisings and obstacles. If we can see past the enemy and continue in the mature love of God, our measure of character will be shown. If we can't, our measure of character will still be shown!

> **Bless them that curse you, and pray for them which despitefully use you.**
> **Luke 6:28**

When we determine to win our cities for God, there will be those who will lie about us, slander us, and falsely accuse us. It would take strong character to be able to pray for them, but it takes more than prayer alone to win a city. The beginning of the verse says to "bless them" even before we pray. We must be mature enough to see past the slander and into the victory of Jesus Christ. Character will keep our vision strong.

And unto him that smiteth thee on one cheek offer also the other; and him that taketh away thy cloak forbid not to take thy coat also.
Luke 6:29

This verse isn't always talking about someone physically striking you on the cheek. It is speaking of such strong slander in your presence that only the character of God could leave you standing unmoved. History points out that this kind of slander toward the turn-of-the-century preachers left the accuser sobbing and repenting. The early preachers of America refused to be moved in their character.

Give to every man that asketh of thee; and of him that taketh away thy goods ask them not again.
Luke 6:30

There are some people who will cheat us in the name of the Lord. There are some Christians who lack sadly in character and will try to take advantage of us by association or by finances. We cannot allow the shallowness of another believer to move us off our character.

And as ye would that men should do to you, do ye also to them likewise.
Luke 6:31

Our character prompts us to treat every man as we would like to be treated, whether we ever receive the same treatment from the person or not. We will reap what we sow.

Judge not, and ye shall not be judged: condemn not, and ye shall not be condemned: forgive, and ye shall be forgiven.
Luke 6:37

Oral Roberts once asked me, "Happy, which would you rather have, judgment or mercy?"

I answered, "Mercy." I have never forgotten that.

A person with character is a person with a clear conscience. If we will judge ourselves the minute we know something isn't right, our conscience will not be seared and we will not become callous to the Holy Spirit. Therefore, we will not be judged by others rightfully.

When we have character, we also forgive, because of the spiritual consequences we will reap if we retain any bitterness.

> **Give, and it shall be given unto you; good measure, pressed down, and shaken together, and running over, shall men give into your bosom. For with the same measure that ye mete withal it shall be measured to you again.**
>
> **Luke 6:38**

That is a popular verse when it comes to giving, but the verse does not only apply to finances. It is a spiritual law. In whatever we give, it will be given back to us again in the same measure we gave it.

In reaching a city, our character will be what the people see. The people of the city will not know us personally, but they *will* hear us and they *will* watch us. We may be the only instruments God places before a city to bring it deliverance, to bring it out of traditional bondage, to minister healing to diseased bodies, and to point the people to salvation in Jesus Christ.

The people of the city tell the degree of character a person has according to the wisdom used in a situation. *Character carries with it wisdom and understanding.* All through the Word, we read about situations men and women of God were up against and the faith they used to see themselves and the people through it. Their character got them out of trouble! It was shown by the wisdom, understanding, and faith they used to meet the challenge.

If we will groom our character, God will give us our cities! He knows we will point the way to Jesus Christ through true wisdom, understanding, and the anointing He has placed on our lives because we walk in the character of Christ.

Chapter 4
Diligence

The principle of "diligence" is one of the greatest revelations we can receive as a Christian. Once we understand the basic truths of healing, deliverance, and prosperity, we cannot fully appropriate them without diligence working in our lives. The same is true in reaching a city for God. It is an easy thing to go out and announce "God wants our city," but it is another thing to keep that revelation alive ten or twenty years down the road.

Reaching a city for God involves more than a proclamation or crusade for soul-winning. Do not misunderstand — soul-winning is an imperative part of reaching a city; but it is only the start of it. We cannot fully saturate a city by thinking that the people coming forth in an altar call "took it." In order for those people to be effective in their city, they must be steadily taught and trained to take hold of the principles of the gospel.

There are many godly qualities that shape and groom our character, and we must develop them to fully reach a city for God. One of those qualities, the spiritual force of diligence, could mean the difference between failure and success. When we grasp the principle of diligence, we will cause our proclamations to become ongoing, living realities.

Keep thy heart with all diligence; for out of it are the issues of life (Proverbs 4:23). We could paraphrase the verse this way: "Set a constant guard or watch around your heart because out of it will flow the source of your life." Although diligence applies to every spiritual law written in the Word of God, I want to deal primarily with diligence in reaching a city for God.

Once we get the understanding that God is a God of cities, we must *set our hearts to diligence*. We must become aware of the fact that we are instruments God has strategically placed in that city to turn the people toward His goodness and mercy. Then, when we understand that fact, we must keenly guard what we see and hear, knowing whatever we put inside us will eventually come out of our mouths.

Paul was speaking to the Roman believers regarding spiritual character when he said, **...he that ruleth, with diligence** (Romans 12:8). When God commissions us to reach our cities, we are in a position of spiritual authority that cannot be taken lightly. It is a serious thing to proclaim we are "reaching our city for God." We no longer become "the church on the corner."

Church leaders and believers alike will have the same commission to lead their city by spiritual diligence. Diligence is not careless, hasty, or rushed. It is steady and paced. Diligence is not haughty or lofty. Diligence *works*.

Years ago, God spoke to my heart and asked me what diligence meant to me. I thought I knew the answer. I said, "Well, Paul spoke to Timothy and told him to preach the Word and be instant, diligent, in season and out of season," and that was all I knew about it. That wasn't the answer. God let me know that unless I found out what the spiritual principle of diligence held, neither I nor the people around my ministry could ever accomplish the work He had placed before us.

Diligence is of the same importance as the measure of character and faith in our lives. They all work together. We can't have one without the other. If one ministry is growing by leaps and bounds and another isn't, look for the principle of diligence. If one person is prospering and another is losing every dime he makes, diligence is the core. That is why some people who have only been Christians a few years are more mature than some who have been Christians for twenty years. Diligence will promote us.

That is exactly what Paul was telling the leaders and believers in Romans, chapter 12. By telling the people to be diligent in the ministries given to them, he was saying they should be "earnest, businesslike, and eager" in taking care of the things entrusted to them.

It is sad to point out that many ministries today do not fulfill the plan of God for their city because they lack these qualities. The world has seen the church as a sloppy, unbusinesslike "crutch" that takes their money and baby-sits them when they feel weak. They think ministers live a life of leisure and are on a constant vacation. Unfortunately, the church has not kept their understanding of diligence, or the world might see us differently in that respect.

To win a city for God, ministries must be businesslike and earnest in their dealings. We can never establish the principles of Christ on a large scale if we are slothful and careless. The church or ministry office isn't a "free-for-all." The ministry office should be run like a business, because it is one. We should be businesslike in representing our operations and transactions, showing excellence in character.

When money is entrusted into a ministry, the ministry must be diligent to apply the funds where they are intended to go. Worldly businesses are not slothful in their salaries or purchases — neither should the church be. As a matter of fact, the world should pattern their methods after the diligence and excellence of the church. A Christian businessman should be the finest example in the business community.

Godly Diligence and Driving Diligence

A diligent person seeks to understand their mission "inside and out." They carefully watch over their task, cutting off excess and slothfulness. When God tells them to do something, they must do it with all their might. They are eager and *exact* to fulfill His plan.

We can't be slothful or lazy and expect to do much for God, especially in being an example before our cities. Notice how Paul begins to instruct us in Hebrews 11:6: **Without faith it is impossible to please him.** Too many times, we stop after the first part of the verse; but look at the last part of the same statement: God is a **rewarder of them that diligently seek him.**

The last part of that verse points out three important things: *reward, diligence, and seeking the things of God.*

There is a *godly diligence* to know His ways, and there is a *driving diligence* to do "our own thing." Scripture says God is a rewarder of those who are diligent "to seek Him." Those who seek to do their own thing have a driving diligence that usually ends in destruction. The only rewards we can see from this type of diligence are manmade awards that will not last.

God will everlastingly reward our efforts if we are consistent in taking care of *His* business. Diligence reveals our priorities, because we will do first what is most important to us. That is why we must constantly be seeking Him and doing His will.

Godly diligence also produces exactness and excellence. By being "exact" in our planning and spending, we cut off any loose opening that could cause confusion. But do not confuse spiritual excellence with perfection. Excellence, motivated by faith, produces the power to be a witness. Perfection, motivated by fear, produces pride and arrogance.

Exactness and excellence will cause us to bring godly stability into our cities.

Diligent in Doctrine

Godly diligence will also cause us to continue in the principles of the Word, thereby obtaining possession of reward. *Godly continuance produces reward.*

What are some of the rewards? Peace of mind, revelation, strength, and recognition in order to be a blessing.

> **Preach the word; be instant [diligent] in season, out of season; reprove, rebuke, exhort with all long-suffering and doctrine. For the time will come when they will not endure sound doctrine; but after their own lusts shall they heap to themselves teachers, having itching ears; And they shall turn away their ears from the truth, and shall be turned unto fables. But watch thou in all things, endure afflictions, do the work of an evangelist, make full proof of thy ministry.**
> **2 Timothy 4:2-5**

"To be instant" in this passage could be paraphrased this way: "Make an effort to be prompt and earnest in every activity of the gospel." That important phrase is the one difference between an ordinary and an excellent Christian. It will be hard for the people of a city to believe our words if we never show up on time for work or an activity of the church.

People respect the person by whom they can set their watch. A person will respect someone who is diligent to do what they say. When a leader makes an announcement of a particular project, the people know it will be completed, because that ministry seeks to be businesslike, earnest, eager, and diligent in the things of God.

As the people of a city watch our lives and see that we are diligent to do what we say, they will readily believe us when they need help. It will be easy for them to see that God is a God of His Word because His people are.

According to 2 Timothy 4:2-5, diligence in the Word of God will keep us from false doctrines. The key phrase is found in verse 2: "in season and out of season."

The "In" Season

When it is the "in season" to do a particular work for God, the faith and energy level are high. It is important to be anchored diligently in the Word because it is an active "season" or time. "In season" can almost feel like a whirlwind; therefore we must stay diligent in the full counsel of God, or we can become weary by the activities surrounding us.

We can never become too busy to pray and intercede, or to exhort and judge ourselves according to the Word. It is imperative at this time to remain "exact" in the things of God. Spiritual diligence can bring that security. If we become too involved in the progression surrounding us to remain diligent in the principles of the Word, then we are heading for trouble.

Spiritual diligence keeps our spirits sharp in cutting off excess or looseness.

The "Out" of Season

Notice Paul says to remain just as diligent in the "out of season" as well. "Out of season" is the time when nothing *seems* to be happening, and we are still doing what God told us to do ten years earlier. Every day can feel the same, and if we do not maintain spiritual diligence, we can get into a trap of thinking "we are accomplishing nothing." A person must be careful then not to take the vision of someone else and make it their own.

When a person is bored or discouraged they are more susceptible to "winds of doctrine" because they did not remain diligent in the principles of the Word. *Deception comes in the form of spiritual things, not worldly things.*

The aim of deception is to draw a Christian away from the simple truths of God. Situations and "revelations" could tempt us to veer from our original instruction if we become frustrated or bored. That is why we must be diligent in the Word to stand against the "wiles" of the devil, as Paul talked about in Ephesians 6:11.

Temptations are obvious, but a wile comes as a scheming lure, hidden to draw us away and deceive us. "Good" ideas are not always "God's" ideas. The "supernatural" is not always "spectacular." How can we tell the difference?

Jesus taught us throughout the New Testament that when we operate in the true supernatural, the work will always point to God alone, no matter how spectacular it seems. We must continue to remain diligent in the Word of God and *examine our motives.* If we are obedient to the original vision given to us, and are diligent to glorify God and not ourselves, God will add to it in His perfect timing.

Paul exhorts us to stay just as eager and diligent when it seems we are going nowhere as we were when we "felt" like we were doing something. Our godly diligence will keep us from deception, which always leads to destruction.

Remember that diligence produces *stability.* Stability and steadfastness are not *always* exciting, but *they are spiritually active.* If we are diligent to follow the Word of God, our doctrine will remain stable and steady to finish the course set before us.

Diligence and Money

In reaching our cities for God, money is involved. Money is not an evil thing. Money is only a piece of metal or paper. The only good or evil involved with money is in the hand of the person who holds it. The wrong intentions of a person's heart make the use of money evil. Right intentions can produce godliness in the use of it.

The heathen of the city, as well as the believers, will watch how money is talked about and handled. We shouldn't be embarrassed about the use of money in operating a ministry. We need money to get the gospel out into the earth. The *preaching* and *accepting* of the gospel is free, but it takes money to *get* a preacher there to preach it, teach it, and train the people. It takes money to *keep* the preacher there to minister and be an example to them.

You may think, "Heaven doesn't need money," but we're not in heaven yet. We are on the *earth* to saturate it with the gospel, and the system of the earth operates by the use of money. The larger a vision we have for our cities, the more money it will take. That understanding should cause godly people to rejoice, not criticize.

> **He becomes poor who works with a slack and idle hand, but the hand of the diligent makes rich.**
> **Proverbs 10:4 AMP**

In reaching our cities for God, we must be industrious and determined in the use of money. We can never complete the vision God sets before us if we deal with a slack or idle hand. If we are industrious and diligent with the use of money, God will send the best deals to us.

Result of Diligence

In the vision for the city of Little Rock, our people grasped the opportunity God gave us for a Christian television network — despite the tremendous opposition and difficulties we faced. Starting the first, full-powered Christian television station in the state of Arkansas was a monumental feat.

The obstacles that surmounted us seemed almost overwhelming at times. Some of the citizens of the state fought ferociously against the station. Even a member of Congress became involved against us. Approximately 22 objections, from the Federal Aviation Authority, farmers in the area, local businesses, and even a U.S. Senator, were given opposing the television tower. Technical professionals quoted time after time that it would cost between 3 to 4 million dollars to operate a fully-powered station.

In spite of these obstacles, the staff and the people *never* gave up on the promise God had given to us. Through diligent and exact planning, Channel 25, a 4.3 million-watt television station, went on the air in Central Arkansas for a little over 1.4 million dollars; and the FCC approved the tower site in spite of the objections opposing it.

The opposition didn't stop there, however. Just because we were on the air didn't mean the city rejoiced. The cable companies wouldn't give us the time of day. At first only one city would put us on their cable system. Great sacrifices were necessary from all of us to continue operating the station.

For four years after we were on the air, the people continued to *diligently* work, pray, and believe what God had promised. When God says something is going to happen — *it does.*

Then the "Must-Carry" Bill of 1992, although vetoed by the President, was passed by an act of Congress that ordered all cable systems to carry local full-time television stations on their network. Within three months, Channel 25 was aired into over 60 cities around the state and our audience was increased ten times.

Those four years of constant diligence in our people instilled industrious determination. The staff of the television station learned the art of delegation and how to work out technical difficulties themselves. Their continued diligence produced results. Now, out of seven local stations,

Channel 25 is one of two that operates 24 hours a day, continuously teaching the Good News.

We have a second television station, Channel 26, in Hot Springs, Arkansas, saturating the western half of our state with the gospel. Other stations will follow. We must continue to be diligent and industrious in the vision God gives to us. If we are idle or slack with the funds given into the ministry, we can never hope to accomplish His plan in the earth. God will give opportunities to His people, but we must be diligent and businesslike to follow His plan.

Because our property is on a hilltop in Little Rock, a cellular telephone company approached us. They negotiated with us to erect their cellular tower on our property, because of the high location. Their 150 foot tower cost them approximately $200,000.

We agreed to the erection of the tower on our property under the following terms: Their company pays us for the use of our property, furnishes our television network with portable phones, and at the end of the lease, we will own the tower. They agreed. They also engineered the pole to enable us to add two more microwave dishes.

God has a plan for every city on earth! He has placed His people within that city to fulfill it. God's Word is true and we can experience the benefits of reaching a city if we are diligent and faithful to believe Him.

Chapter 5
The City and the Tithe

Our assignment in the city of Little Rock is very important to our people as a whole, and they put their money behind it. Since the inception of Agape Church, our people have sought to know God in every avenue of His Word, including the area of finances. It would be very hard to attend our church regularly and not have an understanding of the tithe and offering. As a result, the people are beneficiaries of the promises of God and continue to be a blessing to their city.

I do not know personally who tithes and who doesn't in our church. That is between them and God, but I *have* learned a very important lesson. People must have an understanding of why money is important in the kingdom of God, or they won't give and they won't be blessed. If we haven't learned something, we will not be able to walk in it.

We cannot learn the benefits of healing for our bodies if we are not taught it. The same is true for deliverance, salvation, prosperity, intercession and so on. If people don't know how or why they should tithe, if they don't know the blessings of tithing and the curses of not tithing, *it is only because they have not been taught.*

In order to turn our cities toward God, we must understand and teach the principle behind the tithe and the offering. A leader who will not teach the people on tithing is a leader who will be judged before God, because they neglected to teach the Word.

Tithing Is New Testament

In Luke 11:42, Jesus admonished the Pharisees because they had neglected the other principles of God and were relying on their tithes alone for proof of their righteousness. He is instructing that, yes, it is very important to tithe — but remember the whole counsel of God along with it.

Paul taught the Corinthian church the same principle he had previously taught the Galatians. (1 Corinthians 16:1,2.) He was consistent in teaching that each one should bring a portion of how God had prospered them into the church on the first day of the week. Then, in Hebrews 7, the Holy Spirit tells us how Abraham gave tithes to a priest of the Lord, Melchizedek, in his day. In verse eight, the book goes on to instruct us in this day:

And here men that die receive tithes; but there he receiveth them, of whom it is witnessed that he liveth.

Although we give our tithes to ministries, we live under a spiritual covenant today. The Bible clearly says that Jesus Himself receives the tithe as "worship" when we give into ministries. Tithing is primarily a matter of the heart.

In our church, we lift our tithes and offerings toward heaven and acknowledge that Jesus credited our giving to His account. We are diligent to worship the Lord in our giving.

We don't have bags or boxes by the back doors for the people to place money in if they liked the service. We have "buckets" that are passed down each row of pews. When the buckets are passed among the people, we don't have special singing, music, or frivolous talk attempting to distract the "pain" of giving money to the work of God.

As the people place their money in the bucket, they lift their hands toward heaven, thanking God for the ability to be a blessing according to His Word. They open their hearts and lives to receive the benefits of His promises as they were diligently obedient to give.

The receiving of tithes and offerings is a part of our worship service. Immediately following praise, worship, and prayer, we continue to honor and worship God in the area of finances. The people as a whole have an understanding that the tithe is holy to God, and it is holy to them as well.

As a result, God has blessed the people. He has given them the jobs, the promotions, the increase, the new homes, the babies, and the godly marriages they desire. Godly schools are built. Godly teachers come in to teach and train the children. The children grow up in a godly, educational atmosphere and then go out to affect the world in a positive manner.

Television stations are built and purchased, allowing the love and goodness of God to minister into broken and troubled homes. Then more people come in and receive instruction and it begins all over again.

Once the people understand that the principle of tithes and offerings is for *today* and begin to diligently follow this principle, they begin to experience an ongoing love affair with God. Tithing is a New Testament order.

Tithing and Giving

Remember, reaching a city for God is not a "proclamation," it is a "lifestyle." To win a city in the name of the Lord, we must seek to be well rounded in the full counsel of God. A part of that counsel is in the difference between the tithe and the offering. Malachi 3:8 says we can rob God if we don't do both.

Tithe comes from the word "tenth." (See *Strong's Exhaustive Concordance of the Bible*, #4643.) Because the number *ten* symbolizes the meaning of "government, responsibility, law," when we tithe we establish God's covenant and His law on the earth. Through tithing, the avenue of our faith, we give Him full liberty to prove His Word in earthly circumstances.

To understand the "backbone" of reaching a city, we must understand the structure of the tithe. Let's examine three laws:

Natural Law (gravity)

Civil Law (government)

Spiritual Law (tithing)

If we have common sense, we will not defy the law of gravity. If we have respect, we will obey the speed limit. If we have spiritual understanding, we will know the tithe establishes the rule of heaven in our lives. It is wisdom to say that to win and keep a city for God, all three laws must be followed.

Abraham began the tithe. (Genesis 14:18-20.) In all of his increase, he gave God 10 percent of it. Abraham set the precedent for mankind in the area of tithes. Later, under the Law of Moses, tithing was mandatory. (Leviticus 27:30.)

Under the New Covenant, tithing is a privilege. If we are wise, we will receive that spiritual benefit and set the order of things surrounding us through our tithes.

What does tithing do? It puts God first. It acknowledges Him as the Most High God. If God is not first in our finances, He will never be first in our lives — and He will never be first in our cities.

Too many times we think of spiritual things as something we "have" to do, and we end up in bondage. God doesn't want it that way. God didn't *make* Abraham give Him a tithe. Abraham went to God and said, "You are the Most High God, Deliverer of all my enemies. I'm going to give You 10 percent of all my increase."

God was impressed with Abraham's act of worship and blessed everything he set his hand to do. Then in Malachi, chapter 3, God went on to list His spiritual promises to those who loved Him enough to give Him 10 percent of all their increase.

When we tithe, it shows our thankfulness. God is the One Who causes the increase in our lives. He does it because of His love toward us. He is the One Who gives us the breath in our bodies to work and draw a salary. When we show our appreciation, that small 10 percent becomes *holy* to God. As a result, He makes provision for it in our lives over and above what He has already provided.

By understanding that simple truth, we can begin to see how the tithe shows the heart of a man toward God. *Thankfulness must reign in the hearts of people who take their cities for God.*

Tithing is an important avenue by which we introduce the goodness of God to the people of a city, but if we stop there, we are missing the best part. An offering is a "gift" to God. After we tithe the 10 percent, we are to be *good stewards* over the other 90 percent. When we "give" out of that 90 percent, we will see prosperity in abundance. God does not care how prosperous we become. He only cares when prosperity is our main focus or if we begin to covet.

Second Corinthians 9:7,8 says that *every* man should cheerfully give as he purposes in his heart. Then God will make all grace abound toward them that they might have sufficiency in all things. Think of the things that can be done in our cities if the people have a cheerful heart in giving. Offerings, or giving, is a measure of our love toward God.

We do not put pressure on the people to tithe, but we do require they hear the Word and make the decision themselves. If we will embrace the truth behind tithes and offerings, we will be able to abundantly bless the people of our cities through our giving, and turn their eyes toward God.

The Church of the living God will not have one excuse for not fulfilling the plan of God for their cities. If every person who is a believer would tithe, there would be sufficient funds to do every work God placed before us.

Tithing to Your City

In a previous chapter, I mentioned how during Christmas, we took a tithe to our city by blessing the Little Rock Police Officers with a check for $10,000.

While reading one day in Deuteronomy 26, I noticed they took tithes to their city (that was the spirit of what was happening in that particular chapter). They took tithes to the Levites, the ministering tribe, the stranger, the orphan, and the widow so that they could eat within the "gates," or the city.

At this particular time, our police had been asking the city for a raise and the city refused. I felt very strongly impressed to help them. As I was reading Romans 13:1-7, I noticed that city officials or authorities are "ministers for our good" (verse 4). So, I asked God if we could give a tithe to our police officers and treat them like Levites. God said I could.

We rented the city auditorium, worked with the Union Rescue Mission, and invited all these folks to a church Christmas party. During the program, we handed out groceries to the homeless, distributed gifts to the orphans, and presented a check for $10,000 to the chief of police. Each officer received a check for $33 to represent the thirty three years of Jesus' life on the earth. We simply wanted our police to know there was a group of people who loved them and cared for them.

A few years earlier, we had started the "Peace Officers Prayer Partner Program" in our city, where each church member received an officer's name to pray over each day. This act of love toward our city created no small stir. The letters we received were indicative of a group of men and women who were shocked, but grateful. It also began a relationship between the police and our city that has grown stronger every year.

A wonderful man, a Four Square pastor in our city, felt led to resign his pastorate and become the chaplain for the Police Department. Since the city had no money to pay a chaplain, we and some other churches in the city, along with the Fraternal Order of Police, pay his salary. What God has done in our police force is wonderful. The chaplain is loved and respected by the police and the community.

When a police officer is slain in the line of duty, our church is often used for their funeral. The last funeral we had was the most anointed I have ever seen. On the front row sat the mayor, city directors, and city officials. Filling the auditorium were over a thousand law enforcement officers from our city and state.

I cannot describe the awesomeness of these men and women in uniform filing down the aisle to pay tribute to their fallen officer and stopping to hug their chaplain standing at the head of the casket.

The funeral lasted three hours, and I don't think there was a dry eye in the house. As the five-mile funeral procession passed through the streets of Little Rock, it really touched our city.

What's happening? We are creating a God-consciousness in our City — and it all started with a tithe.

Chapter 6
Integrity

Let integrity and uprightness preserve me; for I
wait on thee.

Psalm 25:21

The body of Christ must have and maintain integrity of
heart to have success with God. We are only fooling
ourselves if we think we can be effective as a witness for
God in our cities without integrity. The outcome of all our
endeavors matters little if there is no honesty of heart.

Strong's Exhaustive Concordance of the Bible, #8537,
defines *integrity* as "completeness, innocence, simplicity."
A biblical definition could be paraphrased this way: "No
compromise where the Word of God is concerned, and
nonstop honesty with God."

In 1 Kings 9, Solomon had just completed the building
of the house of the Lord. In verse two, the Lord appeared to
him and said some very important words. He told Solomon
that His name, His eyes, and His heart would continually
dwell in the house, and He would establish His throne in
Israel forever *if* Solomon walked in integrity of heart
(verses 3-5). In other words, everything depended upon
Solomon's integrity of heart and uprightness.

God will preserve those who walk in integrity of heart. We
can read a good example of how important integrity is to
God in Genesis 20. Abraham, for fear of his life, lied to King
Abimelech and said his wife Sarah was his sister. When
Abimelech took Sarah, thinking she had no husband, God
visited him in a dream and told him he had taken another

man's wife. Abimelech reasoned with the Lord and said, **In the integrity of my heart and innocency of my hands have I done this** (Genesis 20:5). Look at the Lord's response:

Yea, I know that thou didst this in the integrity of thy heart; for I also withheld thee from sinning against me: therefore suffered I thee not to touch her.
Genesis 20:6

Because Abimelech had true integrity of heart, the Lord revealed the error, saving him and the entire nation.

Although Job feared for the fate of his children, thereby allowing Satan entrance, he would not release his integrity toward God. Satan annihilated his possessions, killed his family, and tried to destroy his body; but Job's integrity toward God preserved him throughout the calamity. In spite of what his friends and his own wife said to him, they could not steal his integrity. As a result, God gave Job twice the amount he had before Satan tested him, and he lived to see four generations.

There are two kinds of integrity, integrity of the mind and the integrity of the heart. Because they war against one another, it is very important that we understand the difference between them.

Integrity of the Mind

A person who has integrity of mind does not listen to their conscience or their heart. The mind can always think it is innocent if not renewed by the Word of God. True integrity of mind comes by studying, believing, and standing on the Word.

If we do not feed on the Spirit, we will feed on the flesh. When we feed on the flesh, our mind becomes the predominant feature of our lives, and we listen to it and follow it. The mind seeks its own way at all times. It will find an excuse for whatever is beneficial for it. The mind will always choose the easier way, or what "seems" right.

If we operate in integrity of mind, we will have answers, but they won't be the right ones. The mind always tells God what it will do, never listening to what He wants done. Integrity of mind functions according to what is seen, not what is unseen. A person with integrity of mind may hear the Word of God but then do their own thing.

Lawlessness comes from integrity of mind. There is always a reason for doing what they've done, even if it is contrary to the Word. The mind will always justify, because the person has not learned to listen to their heart.

Integrity of mind creates tremendous pressure on the person. Trying to escape from that pressure, they make excuses for the path they choose because they are either ignorant of the Word or refuse to listen to the counsel of God.

When the mind has precedence over the heart, the person becomes self-deceived. That person has the ability to look straight into the eyes of another and lie because they are deceived by their own thoughts.

Integrity of Heart

Anyone can have integrity of mind, but only a man or woman of God can have integrity of heart. Integrity of heart is nonstop honesty with God. Integrity of heart demands that the mind not carry the person off into deception. Integrity of heart is diligence and excellence in spirit. Only by making the effort to live our lives according to the Word and the guidance of the Holy Spirit can we learn to respond according to the heart.

When we have an ongoing, honest relationship with God, pressure seems to diminish because we have made our choice according to the Word and His Spirit. *Integrity of heart allows God to take the pressure* and leads us into both peace and accuracy.

Integrity of heart protects our emotions and produces stability. When we are honest with God to judge and correct ourselves, then no accusation can hurt us because adjustment has been made. Nonstop honesty with God places us in the "secret place" where there is no condemnation. *Integrity of heart learns how to judge itself without condemning itself.* When we are honest with God and seek to live by the Word, our pathway becomes clear.

Integrity of heart is produced from a relationship in knowing and trusting God. If we will uphold God's Word and obey His Spirit, He will uphold us. We must learn to listen to our heart, follow it, and never compromise the Word in any way. That is true integrity of heart.

Developing Integrity

We all have to learn to stand on our own integrity with God. Growing pains are difficult and sometimes uncomfortable, but they produce great results. A city or nation can never be won until we learn to develop integrity of heart.

The core of integrity is trusting God. We must learn to groom ourselves by believing the Word of God. Then, as we obey Him and trust Him with the outcome, integrity grows through our lives no matter the circumstance or situation.

Integrity is demanding but not driving. Integrity demands that the mind and body line up with the Word, no matter how good the justification may sound. Integrity produces skillfulness and excellence in our lives when we diligently apply it.

There are some people who refuse to develop integrity in their lives. These are the ones who are always wanting someone else to do for them. We must learn not to help someone who will not help themselves. To groom our cities for God, we must not destroy the potential of integrity in the life of another, but seek to help them build it.

I have seen some people who are having a hard time trusting God, and I want to help them so badly. Sometimes we just want to give them what they need so the problem will be solved. But if we do not use discernment, we can actually place another person in bondage. If we rush to meet a need, we may be robbing the person of their integrity development.

If God speaks to us to help, then we need to be obedient. However, it is just as important to know when not to help. We should not rush in to meet a need when their character is being developed just because we feel sorry for them. We do not want to destroy the integrity of their heart. God wants to be their Source, and we all have to learn to let Him be.

When I was in the Navy, my ship pulled into port and I called home and asked my father, "Dad, can I borrow fifty dollars?"

He replied, "Don't they pay you, son?"

"Yes, sir."

"Sounds like you need to learn to manage your money."

I learned a lesson right there. My father helped me that day. He raised me right. I learned to be diligent and work it out myself. He didn't destroy my integrity. I wasn't always looking to him when I needed something.

God is the same way. When we learn to stand on His Word and seek His wisdom as needs come our way, then provision is made. Through integrity of heart, God becomes our Source. We won't look to people to meet our needs.

Integrity Promotes

Another important attribute of integrity of heart is in the area of promotion. Promotion does not come from the north, south, east, or west. Promotion comes from God alone.

In Psalm 78:70,71, we read that David, the great ruler of Israel, was once just a shepherd boy tending the flock with all of his ability. The integrity he developed in the pasture caused him to be chosen over all his brothers, though they seemed to be greater in ability. His integrity secured him the job as the king of Israel, and Jerusalem was called the "City of David."

If God has called us to do something, we won't start out at the top. If we are wondering why we are not at the level of success we should be, we need to check our integrity with God. Is our word our bond? Do we have a nonstop, honest relationship with Him? We cannot base our destiny on how we relate to people. We measure our position today against the destiny God has placed before us. The core of all promotion stems from our relationship with *God*.

We can exaggerate or misrepresent ourselves to *people* all day long, and they may never know; but *God* knows.

Two of the greatest hindrances in reaching a city successfully for God lie in the area of exaggeration and misrepresentation. Integrity of heart tells the *truth* and represents itself *accurately. Ministries and lives can be destroyed through misrepresentation.* Integrity of heart speaks loudly in a city. We must seek to represent ourselves by the Word of God according to our present position.

When God instructs us to win our cities, we have to set a pace in order to arrive at the levels and objectives we set for ourselves. We will go higher in life and with God each time we obtain a goal, if we maintain our integrity.

When God first began to speak to us concerning the television ministry, He instructed us to watch what we said. We had to learn to represent ourselves as accurately as possible and to cease from any temptation to exaggerate.

To increase in our integrity, we had to learn to live what we preached and preach what we lived. God bluntly told us, until we got to the place where we realized the importance of integrity, we would not go on television throughout the state.

If we do not maintain integrity, the people of a city will get the wrong idea about us, our church, and ministry. As leaders and believers, we will not go anywhere with God until we get to the next step of integrity.

There is an order to the steps that lead to the top. If we don't take the steps in order, then we are better off to forget about trying to get there. There will always be the temptations of gimmicks and get-rich-quick schemes. People can cheat to get to the top, but they will fall off and become a reproach to everyone who watched them get there.

As long as we do not compromise God's Word or disobey the voice of the Holy Spirit, we will not compromise our integrity. I encourage you to be a believer with integrity of heart and win your city for God in peace and stability.

Chapter 7
People, Principle, and Politics

What exalts a city and a nation? What pulls it down? People are more confused on this subject than any other. In the minds of many people it's the economy of a nation that pulls it up or down. Others think that the correct political party or the right elected officials will exalt a nation.

But God's Word says, *Righteousness* **exalteth a nation: but sin is a reproach to any people** (Proverbs 14:34). We can't fix a nation by just sorting out its economy or fixing its politics. We have to fix a nation by correcting its morality — by changing its character.

When the men who founded this nation walked out of Constitution Hall, Ben Franklin was standing there. They respected Mr. Franklin as a statesman and a man of wisdom. They asked him, "Ben, what do we have? A democracy or a republic?"

He looked at them and answered profoundly, "You have a republic — if you can keep it."

Over the last 200 years, we have been losing our republic. We are diminishing into a democracy. There are many people who will be confused by that statement. They say, "I thought we were a democracy!" No, we were a republic, but we have degenerated into a democracy.

A *democracy* is rule by majority. A *republic* is rule by law. Our nation has become ruled by men of majority, not by law. We *have* laws, but we are not ruled by law. We even have a group of men and women who are called Supreme

Court Justices who are to *uphold* the Constitution. However, as the old saying goes, "Beauty is in the eye of the beholder." People *interpret* something according to their own philosophy, their own idealism, and their own beliefs.

What about separation of church and state? There is no such thing. Ungodly secular humanists and journalists have caused the people of this generation to interpret the Constitution of the United States in that manner. There is no such statement in the Constitution, the Declaration of Independence, or any other official document of this nation. The only thing that is even closely related to that term in the Constitution states, "Congress shall make no law establishing religion."

Separation of church and state is a myth. It simply does not exist, but the Supreme Court's improper interpretation of this statement has hampered this nation for almost a generation.

All of our founding fathers were godly men. They did not write the Declaration of Independence or the Constitution to be misinterpreted by ungodly people. Our founding fathers were men of principle.

That is why our nation needs a harvest. We must, through the gospel of Jesus Christ, bring the nation back to the center point of principle. We must be people of principle to our cities and to our nations. We must vow to live according to principle, not pressure.

People of Principle

God has always intended for His people to be a people of principle. The writer of Hebrews states, **For when for the time ye ought to be teachers, ye have need that one teach you again which be the *first principles* of the oracles of God; and are become such as have need of milk, and not of strong meat** (Hebrews 5:12).

60

It was God's design for us to learn the basic principles on living successfully and go on from there. He never intended for us to sway from right and wrong, making excuses for it by our own interpretations.

It should alarm us to hear people saying, "I don't care about character. I don't care about morality. I don't care about family. I don't care if a person is honest. All I care about is money and economics. What's going to put money in my pocket...how am I going to benefit...what am I going to get out of it...how can I justify something to relieve all this pressure?" Instead of bumper stickers that say, "If it feels good, do it," they should read, "If it's *right*, do it."

Therefore leaving the principles of the doctrine of Christ, let us go on unto perfection; not laying again the foundation of repentance from dead works, and of faith toward God.

Hebrews 6:1

To paraphrase the beginning of that verse, we could say, "Let us build from the basic principles of Christ and go on into maturity." The word *principle* means, "foundation, the essential character of anything, general truth, settled rule of law, principles of contract." (See *Webster's New Collegiate Dictionary*, 1960.)

The preaching of the gospel and teaching of the Bible should be the "settled rule of law" governing our lives if we are to ever effect our cities and nations for God. What is right is right, and we should never sway from it. That is what our mission is all about.

We must produce people of principle by preaching the gospel and making disciples. We can never reproduce godly principles if they are not already inside us. Our opinions will not last. Only the Word of God is eternal and foundational.

Laws do not change people. Only the *gospel* changes people. It is good to have laws. We need jails, prisons, and

61

sentences, but they are a "Band-Aid effect." *Only people of principle will change the world.*

The mission of the church is to *change the hearts of men*, not to get all caught up in lawmaking and exposing government. Jesus consistently taught the principles of heaven, and those who received them were changed. If we seek to be people of principle and change the hearts of people, then eventually a *changed heart* will be instrumental in changing the laws.

Leaders of Principle

Genesis 18:19 is a powerful verse that explains how God sees a man of principle and what He will do for that kind of society. Speaking of Abraham, God said:

> **For I know him, that he will command his children and his household after him, and they shall keep the way of the Lord, to do justice and judgment; that the Lord may bring upon Abraham that which he hath spoken of him.**

1. Leaders of Principle Are Known By God

Because Abraham was a man of principle, he was a familiar friend to God. God said, *"I know him; I recognize him; I observe him and he is My friend."* For God to *know* the leaders of a nation is very important. For someone to say, "I know God" is one thing; but for God to know *them* is a whole other subject.

God will recognize people of principle because they believe in and carry out His heart. God knows each person by name, but for Him to be familiar and intimate with us, we must think and talk as He does. We are not intimate with people who don't share our interest, purpose, or belief. God is the same.

2. Leaders of Principle Command Their Children

Abraham, a man of principle, set the example by teaching his children to live exactly as he lived. Abraham never said, "Do as I say, not as I do." What was good for him was good for his children.

One problem we have in our cities is that we have lost our "father figures." There are not enough godly fathers who set examples, because we have lost principle in our lives. The Bible says that men must set the principle in the families.

Men are to raise their children and be men of character. If the man no longer lives with his wife and children, he should support his children financially. The government shouldn't have to set laws to make a man pay child support. Men should be men of principle and take care of the children they helped bring into the world. That is one of the reasons we have "gangs."

Gangs are substitute families, trying to make up for the fact that a young person never had a father figure of principle in the home. Young people join gangs because, for once in their lives, they feel like they can belong to something and be important to someone.

Part of the reason we have lost "father figures" is because of wrong television programming. Foolish sitcoms make light of fathers today, because a new generation who have been raised without principle are writing those programs.

To reach our cities and nations for God, godly men and godly fathers must return to the forefront and take their rightful place. We must have fathers of principle like Abraham.

3. Leaders of Principle Keep the Way of Justice and Judgment

A society of principle will keep justice and judgment. *Justice* is "rightness and moral virtue." (See *Strong's Exhaustive Concordance of the Bible*, #6666.) *Judgment* is "verdict, sentence or degree, penalty to suit the crime." (See *Strong's Exhaustive Concordance of the Bible*, #4941.)

If a person has done wrong or committed a crime, justice and judgment must be carried out. Part of the reason people do not fear the law today is due to abuses of the appeal system. Even if a person has committed a crime punishable by death, he knows he has the chance to get out of it because his attorney can appeal the verdict.

If we will be a society of justice and judgment and enforce the penalty that fits the crime, there will be less wrongdoing in our streets. If we will be a people who embrace moral virtue and stand for what is right, our cities will be more peaceful.

4. Leaders of Principle Are Blessed By God

God is a good God and He honors people of principle. When we adhere to what is right, we allow God to bring to pass what He has promised in our cities, nations, and the world. This is what we stand for, and we can see the generation "turn around" that is taking place worldwide. We must be people of principle to give God the avenue to bring His goodness into the earth. This is the principle of the gospel.

The Rightful Government

During the last ten years or so, we have had a move to place Christian people in government. We should be involved in the political process and in government, but we should never forget the true mission of the church.

We have to understand that civil government, civil authority, and civil law were all God's idea. We can read that in the Bible. (See 1 Peter 2:13,14.) God established civil government, and within that government, He established civil authority. Civil authority was to legislate civil law.

Why did He do this? He knew there would be people in the earth who would not submit themselves to God. In order to *protect* the godly and to *punish* the wicked, He instituted civil government.

Civil government was to be under God and His authorities. That didn't just mean the President, the Governor, the law enforcement, the Mayors, and so on. It meant *all* who are in authority, including the five-fold ministries (apostle, prophet, pastor, teacher, evangelist).

The five-fold ministries are not only God's gifts to the church but they are also His gifts to the nation. Although the five-fold ministries were also to be involved in civil government, their main mission was to preach the gospel. They were to produce well-rounded citizens, or people of principle.

There have been some well-meaning leaders who have become sidetracked in their quest to change a city or nation. In the shadow of an ungodly government, they have been pricked in their hearts to bring about change. However, in their zeal some have forgotten their first purpose — *to preach the gospel.*

They have become politically engulfed in mind and motivation. Once strong churches, some are now only focusing on political issues and platforms. They have changed their "gospel agenda" into a "political agenda." Some churches think the mission of the church is to be totally political.

The Bible says in Proverbs 11:1, **A false balance is abomination to the Lord; but a just weight is his delight.** It is good to know the issues at stake and to be individually involved, but it is better to know the rightful balance in remembering our mission. The purpose of the church is to change the hearts of men through the preaching of the gospel and living a life dedicated to principle.

Changing a Nation

Although we are in the Church Age, the Age of Grace, many nations are suffering self-inflicted calamities because of their sin. Sin is a reproach to a nation, and a nation can be hurt by sin just like an individual can be hurt by sin. Sin carries with it the recompense of its reward.

Politics never has and never will change a city or a nation for God. Men have tried it in America for over 200 years, and it's still not working. God doesn't operate that way. He operates according to His Word. His plan for every nation is set forth in Proverbs 29:2, **When the righteous are in authority** [or leadership], **the people rejoice: but when the wicked beareth rule, the people mourn.**

Notice that when the righteous are in authority and righteousness increases, even the sinners will rejoice. They will rejoice, not *because* righteousness is increased, but *when* righteousness increases. Why? Through a vehicle of righteousness, God is able to blanket the nations of the earth with His provision and everything gets better.

The world is not pleased when a Christian is elected to a civil office, but they are pleased when the quality of their life improves. Some of them won't know why, but they will rejoice because goodness and provision have increased in the earth. When righteousness is increased, God will exalt His nation and all citizens will live and enjoy the good life.

What does it mean to bring righteousness on the scene? We are not talking about a religion forcing everyone to go to church. God doesn't do that. We are not talking about self-righteousness. What we are talking about is two things you can do to change your nation and turn it around.

First, intercede in prayer for those who are in authority. We will talk about this subject in greater detail in Chapter 9, but it is the first thing that must be done to accomplish any work for God. It is the will of God that men and women be saved and come into the knowledge of the truth. Make petitions, prayers, intercessions, and give thanks for all men. (1 Timothy 2:1,2.)

Intercede for those in leadership who are in an eminent place. This includes intercession for the President, his cabinet and advisors, businessmen, law enforcement officers, ministers, judges, and congressmen. Pray for these people so that you may lead a quiet and peaceable life in all godliness and honesty. When you do, God will become involved in your life, in your city, and in your nation.

Secondly, part of your job in winning your city and changing your nation is to get involved and vote. If you don't vote and you are a Christian, then forget about praying. If you are wondering why we have certain leaders in office, check the polls. It is a proven fact that only *50 percent* of the American evangelical Christians voted in the 1992 political election. *When the church does not make its voice heard, righteousness cannot increase.*

What the world is most afraid of is Christians trying to force their values on everyone. The head of the Arkansas Gay and Lesbian Task Force called me and asked me if our church was going to get politically active. I answered, "As individuals, yes, we always encourage people to get involved with politics and in the community, but as a church, we are called to preach the gospel, and that's what we are going to do. That's what we are here for. That's the assignment of the church."

We are so shallow in our thinking. The issue is not the Democratic or the Republican Party. The issue is a spiritual issue. The issue is righteousness. If we will do what God exhorts us to do, then we will lead a quiet and peaceable life. Godliness and honesty will reign. When righteousness increases, people will rejoice and come into the church. They will get born again, filled with the Holy Spirit, and go into the workplace to be a light and a witness.

Then, as the nation gets blessed, the people will be standing around looking and saying, "My, my, things sure are wonderful lately, aren't they? Crime is down, unemployment's down, wages are up, our environment is cleaner, they are making progress on the national debt...." They start rejoicing.

What is happening? *God is doing what He said He would do.* And when God is involved, the people rejoice. But He is waiting on us. All nations have a desire, and the desire of a nation is shaped by the people of God within the nation. We've looked for God to come into our cities and nations and make everyone a Christian, but God is not going to do that — He never has. He's waiting for His people to pray and obey.

We can't fix a nation by just fixing its economy or its politics. We must fix a nation by changing its morality, its character, and its level of honesty. That is how God commissions us to win a nation. If we will stand in the gap, intercede for authority, be people of principle, preach the gospel, and stand for what is right, God will move on behalf of our cities, states, nations, and the world — and righteousness will exalt the nations!

Chapter 8
Commitment

God is a God of cities. He started with a city, Eden, and He will end with a city, New Jerusalem.

All of God's men were "city builders." They were either strategically placed within a city, or they were told to build one.

In the Bible, we identify people with their cities: the virtuous woman in Proverbs was known in her city (Proverbs 31); Saul of Tarsus; City of David; Simon of Canaan; Jesus of Nazareth.

God spoke to men and women about their cities. Some were sent specifically into a city to preach the gospel and produce people of principle. Jonah was sent to Nineveh to preach repentance. Joseph ruled the nation of Egypt and saved Israel from starvation. Daniel was in the midst of Babylon and was a powerful witness for God as he advised several kings and prophesied the future. Paul was sent into city after city to righteously affect it.

All the men and women of God had a holy fire within them to accomplish their goal, no matter the conflicting doubts or persecution. They had one very important common trait: *commitment*.

> **Commit thy way unto the Lord; trust also in him; and he shall bring it to pass.**
>
> **Psalm 37:5**

Commitment is a word little heard of in society today. The world stresses that a person has a right to get out of a

69

commitment if they so decide. If they are married and suddenly like another person better, the world says it's all right to get a divorce. If a person has given their word to do something and then decides they don't want to do it, the world says they are free to change their minds.

However, in the kingdom of God, commitment is not a shallow thing. It is a principle of life, a spiritual law which is a vital link in obtaining the promises of God's Word.

The word *commit* means "to entrust, to pledge, *to keep* a promise to do something." (See *Webster's New Collegiate Dictionary*, 1960.) There is a big difference between "making" a promise and "keeping" a promise. We must learn that if we are not going to keep a promise, then we must not say that we will.

If our own word means nothing to us, then neither can we believe and act on God's Word. Jeremiah 1:12 tells us God watches over His Word to perform it. Commitment is a holy thing to the Lord, and it should be holy to His people. *As believers and leaders, we must learn to develop commitment or the body of Christ will be severely hindered.*

When a person is committed, it doesn't make any difference what kind of trouble comes. If they are committed in heart, they will stay and continue on.

Commitment is exactly what constitutes a marriage vow. It keeps the marriage together, no matter what difficulties or aggravations come along. When we make that vow, we are committed for life. We recognize there is scriptural reason for divorce, but often even believers divorce for nonscriptural reasons, because they do not understand commitment. If we can't keep our word to our marriage partner, then there is no commitment to the children, the pressures, or the financial needs.

The same is true in following God and His vision for a city. If there is no commitment and continuance in it, then there is no patience in obedience, finances, or the training and fellowship of the people. *Our lifestyles represent the degree of commitment we have toward God.*

Commitment allows us to retain the confidence in what God has ordained for us to accomplish.

Once a commitment is made, *choice* is gone. There is no more deciding whether to do something or not. Changing our minds is no longer a factor. The "doing" of the commitment is what becomes important.

We must learn to avoid anything that comes to distract or take us away from our commitment. When we make the commitment to reach our city for God, every obstacle imaginable comes to distract us. The key to the heart of God and to commitment comes in the form of *continuance*.

Continuance

There is one difference between an overcomer and a person who loses out to weariness, error, or wrong doctrine. The difference is simple yet difficult. That one difference is *continuance*.

In 2 Timothy 3:14, we are exhorted to "continue" in the things we have learned. One reason people don't continue in the things of God is they have never learned them. Just because we have heard a principle of God doesn't mean we have learned it. It is one thing to *hear*. It is another to learn and *continue* in what we've heard. The Bible says faith comes by *hearing* and *doing*. *When we learn something, it becomes a part of us.*

We live in changing times. Things are changing around us every day. However, one thing never changes — God and His Word. Yet there are always "new" doctrines, "new" revelations, and "new" versions popping up. Do they line up with the Word, or were they invented by people who were bored with continuing in the things they had learned?

Second Timothy 3:15 exhorts us to *know the Scriptures* so we will be wise. We cannot get caught up in the fast changes around us. We must be stable and continue in the Word. Then God will open the doors, and we won't have to be concerned about the future.

Continue means simply to "keep doing it." The Bible doesn't say, "Continue as long as things work out for you." The Bible says to *continue in what you have learned*.

We do things continually in the physical. We have to *continue* cutting our hair, *continue* cutting the grass, *continue* bathing, *continue* washing our clothes, and so on. If we stop doing those things, we become a reproach. The same is true in the spiritual realm. We must *continue* in what we have learned from the Word of God and continue seeking and obeying the Holy Spirit in order to be successful.

When God has given us a mandate in our cities, we must learn to continue in what He has told us whether it is "exciting" or not. The same is true with commitment. "Liking" something has nothing to do with commitment.

Continuance keeps reality around us. We must make sure we are in the *right* place and doing the *right* work. Fantasy always promises but never delivers. Magic is when something happens without a price. We have to pay a price to continue in the vision of God.

God wants actuality in His people, and that takes work. We cannot say we are going to "reach our city" for God and not stay committed to it for the rest of our lives. God expects us to count the cost, and then continue in His promises to obtain the prize.

Continuance causes our lives and hearts to be prepared for the opportunities that come. Continuance builds stability and maturity in our lives, enabling us to fulfill the vision with strength and accuracy.

God will never build on the vision He has given us if we are not able to continue in the principles of the Word we have learned. He could not give us more responsibility because we would be unable to see it through.

God may give us a vision of what He wants ten years down the road, but it takes continuance *today* to get there successfully. For example, an athlete may see the Olympic gold medal down the road, but he has to train and master himself *today* before the *future* can become a reality.

How long do we have to continue? Forever! We need a new mind-set if we are to ever do anything for God in our cities. There is no shut-off time. We don't quit when a prayer is answered. We don't stop when a need is met. Continuance is an ongoing thing. It is a lifestyle. It is forever.

Focus

Mine eyes are ever toward the Lord; for he shall pluck my feet out of the net.

Psalm 25:15

Let thine eyes look right on, and let thine eyelids look straight before thee.

Proverbs 4:25

Focus is the "center-point" from which everything we do emanates. What we focus on determines how we live our lives.

Commitment and continuance cause our *focus* to remain on God and His will for our lives. "Focus" does not come as a gift. It is produced on the inside of us by what we do and how we live. Godly focus comes from daily obedience to and relationship with God.

When we were first starting out in the ministry, my wife Jeanne shared with me a spiritual dream that she had had. She wrote about it in detail in her book, *Learning To Trust God's Faithfulness* (Tulsa: Harrison House, 1995), pp. 70,71:

"In the dream I could see myself standing on the side of the earth and it was in flames. People were running to and fro, screaming and pulling their hair, burning alive. I was standing there on planet earth, looking across a great gulf, and I could see heaven on the other side. It looked to be about two blocks away. I saw Jesus standing on the side of heaven with His hands outstretched toward me. He said, "Come." He had on a long white robe and looked so kind and compassionate, so compelling.

"While looking at Him, wringing my hands, I said, "I want to come but I can't! I will fall if I try to walk. I'll fall!" (There was no way to get to Him but by walking on thin air.) He said, "Put your eyes on Me. Look straight into My eyes and begin to walk. Don't look to the left or to the right. Don't look back and don't look down. Just keep your eyes on Me and you will make it."

"Well, I knew that I didn't want to stay there and burn, so I fastened my eyes on His eyes and took a step, then another, and another. I took one step at a time, one foot in front of the other, with my eyes glued to His. If I had looked away, I would have fallen into outer darkness.

"Finally, I made it to the other side — to Jesus! I threw my arms around Him and wept with such joy. He smiled and welcomed me to heaven. Everything was so peaceful, so beautiful, so magnificent. I saw people smiling and talking to one another and, in the distance, I saw a beautiful golden city. It was so wonderful to be there."

That dream encouraged my wife. She knew from that day on that she would make it, no matter the circumstances. She later found out that Jesus is also the Word. (John 1:14.) By keeping her eyes on the Word continually, not looking back into her past, not looking to the left or to the right, she would successfully fulfill whatever God ordained.

Jeanne learned a powerful truth in that dream: There is no feat that cannot be mastered, no foe that cannot be conquered, if we keep our eyes on Jesus and the Word of God. A life in God is a daily walk, committed and continuing in what we have learned. It is a lifestyle of godly focus. It is never taking our eyes off the truth in the Word, no matter what comes against us.

In 1993, we celebrated 20 years together in the ministry. More than ever before, we see how His dream in the earth can become reality if we continue to stay committed and focused on Him.

Vision

And the Lord answered me, and said, Write the vision, and make it plain upon tables, that he may run that readeth it. For the vision is yet for an appointed time, but at the end it shall speak, and not lie: though it tarry, wait for it; because it will surely come, it will not tarry.

Habakkuk 2:2,3

Vision and focus are akin to one another. Vision is not governed by age. Everyone can have a vision from God to fulfill.

The Bible says in Proverbs 29:18, **Where there is no vision, the people perish.** If the people of a city have no goal or purpose in life, they will self-destruct. Without a godly vision that is declared within the city, the people will be morally corrupt, because there will be confusion and hopelessness.

God's people are the life-giving source to cities. The people of the world need the vision His men and women bring. We must embrace the vision God has spoken into our hearts and seek with all of our might to carry it out.

There are six steps Habakkuk has outlined for us:

1. You must have a vision.

A ship without a rudder goes nowhere. Have you ever seen churches that have the same number of people in them they had 50 years ago? That is a church with no vision. That church is going nowhere and doing practically nothing for God.

We cannot live only "day to day." We must also have a goal in our lives. We must have a plan and work our plan. If God has spoken to you, write it down so it won't leave you. Hold the vision to your heart and make it a part of you. If you don't, God will assume you are not interested in the vision He has given you. He will not waste His light for a city or a nation. He'll take it to a people who are excited about it and who will embrace it.

If you don't have a particular vision, then find a local church that has one and make it your vision too. Be obedient to it, pray for it, and seek to fulfill it with all your heart.

If you are going to reach your city for God, it is your job to keep the vision stirred up. God will never take you to the next step of the vision until the first step has been completed.

2. Make it plain.

Write it down! God didn't say to the prophets, "Speak My words out to the people, and we'll just hope they remember it years and years down the road."

No! Thank goodness He had them write it down, and today we have the *written* Word, the Bible. We have His vision and His plan. God made it plain to us.

I carry a piece of paper and a pen with me. When the Holy Spirit begins to minister to me and tell me something, I write it down so I won't forget it. If God tells me something, I want it to stay fresh in my mind and heart. I want to keep it before me so I won't forget it. Every time I read it, it produces a godly strength and confidence inside me to fulfill it.

When is the last time you have refreshed yourself with the vision God has given you? Making the vision and the words of God plain keeps us focused and motivated to action.

Part of refreshing yourself in the vision and making it plain is repeating it over and over. If you are a leader, post the vision every place in your ministry. Have your staff and your people read it over and over and over. Keep yourself stirred and God will refresh you.

3. Others must share in the vision.

God will bring to you, or place you with, the people who share your goal. At the same time, you must be careful with whom you share the vision. Carry what God has given you with sacredness. A vision is a holy thing.

Proverbs 29:11 says, **A fool uttereth all his mind: but a wise man keepeth it in till afterwards.** The Bible says a fool tells everything he knows to everyone. A fool does not count anything as sacred. A wise man will limit his talk. When a vision is given to a wise man, he understands it is a plan from God and to be guarded until the appropriate timing.

It is also not wise to tell all, because God may have to make some adjustments down the road due to people or circumstances changing. If we alter our vision or goal too many times, people may begin to wonder if we know what we are doing. The Bible says, "Don't tell it all until afterwards." Then, when you "know that you know," tell it.

4. It is for an appointed time.

Don't be weary in well-doing. Don't become discouraged. If God has spoken to you, He *will* bring it to pass.

If things seem to be wrong or are at a standstill, you may have departed from your vision. Either Satan has thrown up a roadblock, or you have strayed from your original instructions.

If we find we have departed from the vision and will listen to God, He'll call us back to center point. If we get stubborn, He'll move on someone to intercede for us until we will listen. If we become prideful or too stubborn, He won't do a thing. Finally, if we stay that way, God will raise up someone else to do the job.

God will never give up on us as His children, but He needs the job to be done. I've seen other churches raised up in cities because the one He originally called got off track and wouldn't do the job.

Everything has a correct timing to it, and timing is based on many factors. You may not be aware of them all, but the point is to trust God and follow His vision exactly as He tells you.

5. Wait for it. It will come.

Continue to be diligent and committed. If we continue to walk down the road He has told us to follow, we will come into our season of fulfillment. Waiting for the vision develops character in all those involved. When one part of the vision is fulfilled, God will give you the next step and the process starts again.

Know with every fiber of your being that *if God said it, it will come to pass.* It will come through you if you will be patient and wait for it.

6. It will speak.

Everyone loves to have a sense of accomplishment, but we can never take credit for the vision. The Bible says the vision speaks for itself.

Every time I go through Tulsa, Oklahoma, and pass by Oral Roberts University, I hear the vision speak, "I AM GOD." The vision God gave Oral Roberts for a Christian university speaks to everyone who drives by it, believer or not.

When we fulfill God's vision, we won't have to go around and brag, "I did this," or "I did that." The vision speaks louder and to more people than we ever could.

Back in 1977, the Lord spoke to me to get ready to go on television. I had no money, no training — nothing — but I wrote the vision down just as He spoke it to me.

By 1993, we were reaching 6,000 square miles of television coverage in the state of Arkansas, 24 hours a day. The vision spoke for itself. You don't have to tell people you are in television if you're on the air. They see you!

Remember, as we seek to win our cities and nations for God, the vision He gives to us will speak for itself. Whether the people respond critically or positively, the vision will speak to them and they will make their choice.

Chapter 9
Strongholds and Cities

But if our gospel be hid, it is hid to them that are lost: In whom the god of this world hath blinded the minds of them which believe not, lest the light of the glorious gospel of Christ, who is the image of God, should shine unto them.

2 Corinthians 4:3,4

It is the goal of Satan to have control over a city. Why? Because a city consists of people. It is his design to blind the minds of the people in that city and to harden their hearts toward God. It is the job of the Christian, through intercessory prayer, to bind the strongman and see the vision of God prevail.

There have been volumes of books written on the subjects of prayer and intercession. This chapter will not deal with the specifics involved in the many aspects, but I want to deal primarily with praying down strongholds and interceding for a city.

When praying for your city, there will be two battlefields you must stand on, the spiritual and the natural.

The spiritual battlefield is in the area of intercessory prayer and binding strongholds. What is a stronghold? A "stronghold" is a lie that Satan has built into the minds of people, cities, and governments that is like a castle or fort, which he garrisons and protects with great diligence. In simple terms, Satan has captured their minds with a great deception.

There can be many strongholds within a city. Some examples are:

1) Leaders in the political and economic realm make ungodly decisions and live ungodly lives.

2) Businessmen use their influence in the community for greedy gain instead of for good.

3) Religious men preach a vain religion, holding people in bondage and strangling the very life of God out of their churches.

4) The occult, perversion, and pornography run rampant.

5) Fatherless and ungodly families are deep in poverty, producing children who commit murderous crimes on the streets.

All of these areas are strongholds Satan has produced within cities. How do these things come about? Through the delegation of demonic forces. In Ephesians 6:12, the Apostle Paul categorizes the rank of evil spirits over cities. He says:

> **For we wrestle not against flesh and blood, but against principalities, against powers, against the rulers of the darkness of this world, against spiritual wickedness in high places.**

The kingdom of Satan has rank and assignment. To better understand the delegation of these evil spirits, we need to realize their sphere of influence. All control and orders come from Satan himself. He delegates through the following:

Principalities — magistrates. These spirits rule primarily over nations. The order of the economy and the government of a nation are the primary concerns of the principality.

Powers — delegates. Evil powers receive their orders from the principalities and carry them out through any sphere open to them. If there is any entrance that will affect a multitude, evil powers will work to their best ability.

Rulers — governors of Satan's realm. The world rulers govern the darkness of this world, holding their prisoners blind lest they should ever see the wickedness and deception they are in.

Wickedness or wicked spirits — carry out the orders of wiles and deceptions. Their target is the church. Their responsibility is deception, doctrines of demons, onslaughts, and fiery darts. Wicked spirits study men and women for entrances to temptation. These spirits open the doors for strongholds in a church body. His design is to grieve the Holy Spirit through the people so the church cannot come into the place God has ordained for it. Every false teacher and ministry comes from this group of evil spirits.

[For further study, see *War on the Saints,* by Jesse Penn Lewis and Evan Roberts (New York: Thomas E. Lowe, 1973) p. 17.]

Through this demonic hierarchy, the plans of Satan are carried out in a city. Entire cities and nations have been held captive because the Christian has been ignorant concerning spiritual warfare over their area.

Rather than see cities and nations continue in this kind of captivity and destruction, God has raised up believers who will stand in the gap and intercede, just like Abraham stood up and did business with God for Sodom and Gomorrah.

Abraham said to God, **Wilt thou also destroy the righteous with the wicked?** (Genesis 18:23). No! Similarly, Jeremiah wept over Jerusalem, and Jonah preached the gospel to Nineveh.

There have always been revivalists, the intercessors, those who would stand between the porch and the altar and weep and cry out to God. There have always been the Charles Finneys, the Evan Robertses, and the Dwight L. Moodys whom God has used to stir nations. John Wesley once said, "God does nothing but in answer to prayer." It has always been the intercessors who have changed the course of our nations.

Satan has no authority to do what he does. He gets by with it because Christians have not made intercessory prayer a focal point in their lives and do not understand the biblical command to pull down the strongholds which hold their city and nation in bondage. These Christians are either lethargic, rebellious, or steeped in religious tradition. They are operating under a lack of knowledge which is destroying them.

Lethargy and Indifference

Lethargy is a dangerous spirit that can entrap entire families and, as a result, entire churches. What is lethargy? It is laziness and indifference — and it is very contagious.

If we are not on guard, it will be easy to fall into lethargy. All churches will have to face lethargic situations. When something is "new," it's always exciting. But the "new" wears off in a couple of years, and then it gets down to the real "nitty-gritty." For example, when a person is born again, it is exhilarating and fervor is high. Then when the "new" wears off, it comes down to a daily maintenance program in their walk with God.

The building of a church is no different. Everyone is excited at the beginning. There are always the projects and the objectives. Then it begins to become a chore to attend the services, because we've worked hard all week. It is hard to remain diligent, but we must see past the local church body and into the people of a city. The world is dying, and only the body of Christ can help them.

Another sign of lethargy is "indifference." One of the main reasons Christians don't get involved in their cities is due to indifference. "Well, I don't care one way or another if we reach the city...if we get that building built...if we go on television...someone else will do it...." The key phrase here is "I don't care." That's indifference, and it's a killer.

As believers, we cannot allow the deception of indifference to entrap us. We must care about people the way Jesus cares about them. We can't be still and we can't be passive. We have to make a difference. We have to go and possess the land. We have to win and train our cities for God.

That's why reaching your city for God is an ongoing lifestyle. It always sounds exciting at first, but then the day-to-day maintenance comes — the standing, the prevailing, the proclaiming, the diligence, and the continuance. We must keep ourselves refreshed through right associations, the Word, and the Spirit. Then we will keep ourselves from a lethargic rut. God's mercies are "new" every morning, and His faithfulness never ends.

It is the job for the Christian who understands that God is a God of cities to diligently stand in the gap for their city. It is God's will to rule in your city, and you can be the vessel who can make the difference. (Read Ezekiel 22:30 and Genesis 18:23-33.)

A Foundation in Little Rock

When we started Agape Church, it began with intercessory prayer. Intercessory prayer is the foundation of our ministry. God said He would deliver the city of Little Rock into our hands for the preaching of the gospel, but we had to use our authority in the Spirit, allowing God a pathway to do what He promised. We continuously pray and intercede for our city and state.

My Senior Associate, Terry Nance, saw a vision one morning while he was in prayer. In the spirit, he saw the evil spirits ruling over the city of Little Rock. Those spirits had a noose wrapped around our city, strangling the very life out of it.

The Lord showed Terry the end results of our intercession. Suddenly, the noose came off of the city, and it was thrown around the neck of the evil spirits, choking the very life out of them instead! That noose symbolized God taking the authority over those spirits as we prayed. God showed us what was happening.

If we are faithful to intercede, the Spirit of God will show us the primary spirits involved in our cities. He will call them by name. However, many times, the major stories throughout a city newspaper will show the workings of the evil spirits involved in that city.

Years ago, traveling ministers would not come into Little Rock to hold their meetings because of the strongholds that were present. William Branham wrote that Little Rock was "the most satanically oppressed city he had ever been in." Another well-known minister said, "The heavens were spiritually black" over our city.

The people of Agape Church took their assignment in Little Rock seriously. They understood it was their responsibility to bring the light of God into their city, and we would *all* be accountable to God for that. Through years of intercession, and because we bound the evil strongholds holding our city in bondage, the atmosphere has changed! The battle will not be over until Jesus returns, but the heavens are now open.

A well-known television evangelist said of his last meeting in Little Rock, "It was the greatest response at the altar for the size of the crowd attending than in any other meeting." Things are changing for the good!

The Natural Battlefield

The natural battlefield is standing against the wiles of the devil. We must hold fast to what we have prayed. Jesus delivered the city from the devil. He has taken the keys of life and death. He shed His blood for the people of the city. His Word will never return to Him void and it will accomplish what it was sent to do.

In the natural battlefield, we must never become weary in believing what we have prayed. If we have prayed the Word of God and we are convinced of His will, then we will see results. Hold fast! If you have prayed for a specific thing but it seems just the opposite happened, acknowledge the facts but speak the *truth*: "Jesus is Lord over my city." The light of God has come into the city, and you are an instrument to proclaim it.

After praying, it is our natural responsibility to guard our minds and hearts from anything that is contrary to the Word of God.

It is not just the leader's responsibility. It is also the responsibility of the body to not allow a stronghold in their church. If you are serious in reaching your city for God, you won't come into the church on Sunday and "park" on a pew for awhile to be entertained. Instead, you will have a vital part.

Christian people should hold sacred their freedom and openness to the Holy Spirit. We must deal with strongholds through prayer, teaching, and holy living. In this way, the body of a local church can guard that church from deception, false doctrine, and false teachers and prophets.

As members of the body of Christ, whatever right-of-way we give to an evil spirit doesn't affect us alone. When individuals allow an evil spirit to seduce and influence them, it affects their family, their church, their community, their city, even their state, and eventually their nation. It produces a stronghold. If we are serious about reaching our cities for God, we can no longer say, "Well, it's my business. I'll yield to whatever I want, to get whatever I want."

That stronghold within a local church will grieve and hinder the Holy Spirit. He will not be able to manifest Himself among the people to save, heal, and deliver as He desires. That is one reason the corporate anointing is so important and so powerful.

Why do some churches lose their influence? They allowed strongholds to build up within the people. The issues were never addressed; they were ignored. As a result, the stronghold built up into such a garrison that the Holy Spirit couldn't budge them or get them to change and go on with the plan of God for their city. As a result, their city would be unaffected until God raised up another work to carry out His plan.

How Strongholds Come

Understand that strongholds come through people. That is how evil spirits rule. The evil spirits introduce and bombard the minds of people with a deception or lie until it captures, or forms a stronghold, in their minds. When there are many people under the control of a stronghold, we can see the effects of it in a city.

If the city is oppressed, the people in it are oppressed. If the cities are free and happy, the Spirit of God has liberty there. Satan's first opportunity, however, is not to come and get into the church. His first opportunity is to get into the *city*. Then he tries to get the evil spirits of the city to come into the church.

If he can oppress the city, he is hoping that oppression will work its way into the church. Then the people of God, who are the only ones with the authority to cast them out, will be held captive. A city and then its churches can be held by greed, perversion, and every evil work.

We know that Jesus saw Lucifer fall from heaven as lightning. (Luke 10:18.) We know Jesus told John in the Book of Revelation that He has the keys to hell and death. (Revelation 1:18.) We know that He received power and authority over Satan, and He gave that power and authority to the church. (Matthew 28:18-20; Luke 10:19; Matthew 10:1.)

We know that Satan and his demons still operate in this world's system. They are going to be here until their "time." (Matthew 8:29.) Some people wonder why Jesus didn't just cast the demons off this planet so we wouldn't have to deal with them anymore. That time will come, but not yet. Until Jesus comes back to establish His kingdom, demon spirits are going to be in this world system.

God was trying to reveal to His church that even though demons are here, they have no power and authority over the believer who uses the name of Jesus. Demons have no rightful authority in our cities unless the children of God allow it.

Fervent intercession will change the course of your city. What is fervency? It is being together as one — body, mind, and spirit. It is being white-hot for God. That means your spirit isn't doing one thing while your mind is thinking of something else. All three parts of you come together as one for the purpose of petitioning God and taking authority over the enemy. James 5:16 says, **The effectual** [unceasing] **fervent prayer of a righteous man availeth much.**

The Authority To Take Your City

God has strategically placed you within your city for a purpose. It was not by chance. It was not by accident. Your place of employment didn't cause you to be there. God sent you there.

When you understand your position with God, it draws confidence and wisdom into you. You are an Ambassador for Christ in the cities and nations of the world. You live on the earth, but your citizenship is in heaven. You are not *of* this world, but you are *in* this world to do a job for God. You are "on loan" from heaven to the world.

You are the righteousness of God in Christ Jesus. You have the authority *of* heaven. When you were born again, it didn't happen just so you could *go to* heaven. It happened so you could be given the authority *of* heaven. That means you can operate in this earth as God operates in heaven.

You have been given, through Jesus Christ (not of yourself), the authority to use His name while you are on this earth. You were predestined by the Holy Spirit to be born when you were born, and to do what you are doing at this time and this place.

By being an Ambassador for God, you are operating under the rules of heaven, not the rules of this world. Therefore, you have the authority to speak the Word of God in your city and it be done. You have the power to bind and loose. Whatever you bind on earth *will be* bound in heaven; whatever you loose on earth *will be* loosed in heaven. Whatever you bind or loose will be backed by heaven's authority.

You have the authority to bind principalities and powers, rulers and wicked spirits, and render them helpless and inoperative in your city. You have that power and that right through Jesus Christ. He placed you on the earth to accomplish His plan.

Purpose to win your city for God and to teach and train others to do the same. When the final day comes, we can then stand before God and give account with great joy.

Chapter 10
Jonah and Nineveh

I recently reread the entire book of Jonah. It is one of my favorite books in the Bible, and even though I have read it many times, I saw some things I had not seen before. It reminded me of the purpose for the harvest: learning to do what God tells us to do.

When God told Jonah to go and cry against the city, that meant *preach*. The book of Romans says, **How shall they hear without a preacher?** (Romans 10:14). The Bible also says that **Faith cometh by hearing, and hearing by the word of God** (Romans 10:17). God told Jonah to go and preach His Word to Nineveh.

Nineveh had been built by one of Noah's grandsons. God's plan was for His men to build cities and allow Him to reign through them, thereby making Him the God of their city.

The division between believer and unbeliever we see in our cities today is not the will of God. The warring between the righteous and the unrighteous was never God's plan. It has always been the will of God for the righteous to rule.

The Bible tells us that when the righteous are in authority, the people rejoice. This has always been and always will be the will of God — for entire cities to serve Him. The city of Nineveh responded to the preaching of one man, and God hasn't changed.

Years ago when God sent me back to Little Rock to raise up Agape Church, He said, "I will deliver the city into your hands for the *preaching* of the gospel." When I first heard the Spirit of God say that, it really didn't mean very much to me. I thought to myself, "I'll write that down." I was astounded by it, but I didn't understand it. I thought, "This would be good for somebody like Billy Graham or Oral Roberts or Kenneth Copeland or Kenneth Hagin — but not for Happy Caldwell."

I didn't think much about God's promise to me at first, but it began to grow and get bigger and bigger on the inside of me. Now, when the Lord asks, "Am I doing what I said I would do?" I say, "Yes, Lord, You are doing it almost faster than I can take advantage of it!" God is delivering the city and the state into our hands for the preaching of the gospel. He is doing His part.

God told Jonah to go to Nineveh and *preach* because their wickedness had come up before Him. Wherever you find wickedness, you'll find preaching, because receiving Jesus Christ as Lord and Savior is the only way people can become righteous. That is why preaching is so important.

Jonah, however, ran the other way. He got on a ship going in the other direction. A storm arose and the people on the ship began praying to their own gods. In the midst of the storm, Jonah was deep inside the ship, fast asleep, trying to get away from what God had said. He didn't want to face what was happening.

The people on that ship knew something wasn't right. They knew this wasn't a normal storm. When they cast lots to find out who had brought the storm upon the ship, Jonah came up with the short stick. They were really afraid when they found out who Jonah's God was! They knew they were going to perish because of Jonah's disobedience.

When I was in the Navy, we were told that a ship out on the ocean is like a city all by itself. If every person on the ship does his job right — you might live. If only one person does his job wrong, it could kill everyone on the ship.

The sailors on Jonah's ship knew that something was wrong with Jonah. That's when Jonah confessed that the storm was his fault, and he asked to be thrown into the sea. In spite of what Jonah said, the sailors tried with all their might to get to land. They wanted to put Jonah off on the shore, but they couldn't, because the storm was fighting them. Finally they had to throw him overboard, and the sea became calm.

God had prepared a great fish to swallow Jonah, and if it weren't for the fish, Jonah would have drowned. A lot of people don't understand that God was actually saving Jonah's life. Once he was in the fish's belly, he started praying.

The only thing God had asked Jonah to do was to go to Nineveh. You have to realize that when God asks you to do something, He's serious. He doesn't just slip up on you one day and say, "Oh, there you are, I've been looking for you." God knows where you are all the time, and He comes to you on purpose because He wants *you* to do something.

The Bible says Jonah cried out to God because of his affliction. He wasn't praying because he had a change of heart. He was praying because he was in worse shape than when he was on the ship. However, God heard him anyway.

When Jonah remembered God, the situation started to change. Things had gotten so bad that Jonah lost control. He couldn't handle it anymore. The pressure was so great that his soul fainted. That's when his spirit reached out and said, "I remember what God told me to do. Now I know what got me into this mess."

That's what the harvest is all about. People must do what God tells them to do. Jonah got a revelation:

They that observe lying vanities forsake their own mercy. But I will sacrifice unto thee with the voice of

thanksgiving. I will pay that that I have vowed. Salvation is of the Lord.

Jonah 2:8,9

God had asked Jonah to preach to Nineveh. When Jonah finally surrendered to His will, God spoke to the fish and the fish spit Jonah out in one big belch. Jonah hit the beach running, and he was heading straight for Nineveh.

When God called me to build a church in Little Rock, we were in the traveling ministry. I tried to tell Him Little Rock didn't need another church. There were already plenty of churches there. I argued with God, and He gave me a grace period, but then the grace for the traveling ministry seemed to stop. There was no money coming in, and I couldn't fill a date anywhere. I might as well have been in the whale's belly. It was miserable.

I argued with God. I didn't want to do it. One time I told Him, "I'm not qualified to do that." He answered (and it was not intended as a compliment), "You sound just like Moses." God wasn't flattering me. Moses argued with God until the time he died. His intercessions stopped the plagues and caused God to repent, but Moses did not argue with God properly most of the time. Neither did Jonah, and neither did I.

Isn't it sad that God has to carry some of us along like little babies? He has to rock us to sleep and pat us on the back to get us to do one thing! He can speak to us in our beds, in our quiet time, or in our prayer time in such a way that nobody else could speak to us — in our inner being. He tells us what He wants us to do, and we just cast it off. Then we go to a meeting and someone prophesies to us, and we shout and scream and get all excited because we heard from God. We actually heard from God way back there on our bed in the night time!

Now what happened to Jonah? The word of the Lord came unto Jonah the second time. Has God ever spoken to you a second time about the same thing? God doesn't usually speak to me more than once or twice about something. And when He speaks to me, it booms around on the inside of me, and the only way I can get rid of it is to do what He says.

God spoke to Jonah the second time, saying, **Arise, go to Nineveh...and preach unto it the preaching that I bid thee** (Jonah 3:2). You must notice that God said, **Preach unto it the preaching that I bid thee.** If ministers could only learn this! God does not tell all ministers to do things the same way. God told me to do things a certain way, and He'll tell somebody else to do it a different way.

People are supposed to do things the way God tells them to do them. If we can learn to do things the way God tells us to, let other people do things the way God tells them to do things, and pray for this one over here and pray for that one over there, and bless this one and bless that one, we'll get the job done and get out of here!

God told Jonah to preach to Nineveh the way He wanted him to preach. Here is what God told him to say, **Yet forty days, and Nineveh shall be overthrown** (Jonah 3:4). That's so simple! Jonah ran from God, got caught in a storm, and was swallowed by a fish to avoid saying eight words!

The Bible says that it's not by our might or power, but by the Holy Spirit that God's will is accomplished. (Zechariah 4:6.) If the Holy Spirit isn't backing us, we can preach an hour and no one will get saved, but eight words directed by God can get a city to receive the Lord. That's why the people of Nineveh believed God when they heard Jonah's message.

Nineveh was a big city. Historians tell us there were approximately 170,000 people there. That's a big city even today. Jonah's message came to the king of Nineveh, and he proclaimed a fast. The people of Nineveh fasted and put on sackcloths. Everyone in the city turned from their evil ways and turned toward God.

God saw that Nineveh repented and He decided not to destroy the city, but that displeased Jonah. Why was he angry? When you realize why, it may shock you. Here we see the pride of the man.

Jonah prayed again, but this wasn't like the prayer he prayed in the whale's belly. In the whale's belly he was praying by reason of his affliction. Now he was praying out of anger. He's "mouthing off" to God.

Have you ever been angry at God? Have you ever complained to Him? Some people are afraid of talking to God like that, but as long as you have integrity and uprightness of heart, you don't have to be afraid. However, if you don't, you better watch out. As long as God knows your heart is right, He'll put up with a little stupidity.

Jonah prayed and said, **Was not this my saying, when I was yet in my country? Therefore I fled before unto Tarshish** (Jonah 4:2). Here is what he was saying: "This is why I didn't do what You asked me to do the first time. This is why I went to Tarshish instead of Nineveh. I knew You were a gracious and merciful God. I knew You were slow to anger and would not destroy the city if they repented."

Can you believe it? He didn't go to Nineveh because he knew in his heart that Nineveh would repent when he preached what God told him to preach and then God would forgive them. That's why he didn't want to go. He wanted them to be punished for their sins.

God's hatred for sin demands punishment thereof, but His love and compassion for people demand salvation. The Word declares the wages of sin are death. (Romans 6:23.) **The fear of the Lord is to hate evil** (Proverbs 8:13). When you say you fear the Lord, you are saying you hate pride and evil just like He does. However, you also have to say that you love the sinner. Now here's where we are in danger, like Jonah, of getting mixed up in harvest time.

We cannot hate the sinner. We have no right to hate the sinner. If we hate sinners, then Jesus can say to us what He said to the sons of thunder when they wanted to call fire down from heaven, "Just burn 'em up, Lord, just kill them all."

Jesus said to them, "Hush up! You don't know what spirit you're of." (See Luke 9:54,55.) The sin demands punishment, but the sinner demands salvation. God loves the sinners and God wants them saved.

In Exodus, Moses stood before God for the sins of the people of Israel, reminding Him of His covenant. The Bible says God repented, but that doesn't mean He changed. It was never God's will to hurt and destroy people. It has always been His will to raise up a people whom He could love through all eternity.

In Ezekiel it says that God was looking for a man who would stand in the gap for the people, but He couldn't find anyone. Let's consider Sodom and Gomorrah. The fact that God destroyed those cities and buried them underneath the Dead Sea is not an indictment against those people.

God went to Abraham and said, "Abraham, what about Sodom and Gomorrah — what are you going to do about it? Abraham stood before God and interceded for the people. God told him that if he found ten righteous, he would spare the city. (Genesis 18:32.) God was looking for a way to spare the city and preserve His people. He was looking for a way to bring in the harvest, but He was bound by His judgment of sin to destroy it.

The indictment of putting Sodom and Gomorrah under the Dead Sea and preserving it so that it would eventually be unearthed for people to see the degradation and the stench of the sin was not an indictment against the people. It was an indictment against the sin.

This is what we forget in the harvest. When you see an old drunk in the street, you may think, "Ah, you lousy bum." Although He hates what the man has become, God loves him. God hates the sin that has enslaved the prostitute in bondage, but He loves the girl. God hates the crime, but He loves the criminal. That's what God was trying to get across to Jonah.

"Their wickedness has come up before Me, Jonah. Go and preach My gospel to them. Go and preach My Word to them." Jonah, in his pride, turned and went the other way. There are times when I would love to have left the church and the ministry because things were difficult. However, I am more committed to God and what He has demanded I do than I am to my own desires.

There will be times when you get hurt and kicked and criticized and hated, and you'd like to say, "Who needs this?" You will be talked about and you'll know it's not true; but the minute you start defending yourself, you'll become just like those who are talking about you. If you ever retaliate, you are done for! The only way to succeed is to walk in a spirit of forgiveness and meekness. Vengeance belongs to God, and you can't help Him out.

Jonah was more concerned with what He looked like than what happened to the people. He goes on to say, **Therefore now, O Lord, take, I beseech thee, my life from me; for it is better for me to die than to live** (Jonah 4:3). Why? He knew the people would repent, then God would repent, the city would not be destroyed, and his prophecy would not come to pass. He had no concern whatsoever for the restoration of the city. He just wanted his prophecy to be right. Jonah's sin was pride when he said, "God just kill me, I don't want to live anymore."

So Jonah went out of the city, and sat on the east side of the city, and there made him a booth, and sat under it in the shadow, till he might see what would become of the city.

And the Lord God prepared a gourd, and made it to come up over Jonah, that it might be a shadow over his head, to deliver him from his grief. So Jonah was exceeding glad of the gourd.

But God prepared a worm when the morning rose the next day, and it smote the gourd that it withered.

And it came to pass, when the sun did arise, that God prepared a vehement east wind; and the sun beat upon the head of Jonah, that he fainted, and wished in himself to die, and said, It is better for me to die than to live.

And God said to Jonah, Doest thou well to be angry for the gourd? And he said, I do well to be angry, even unto death.

Then said the Lord, Thou hast had pity on the gourd, for the which thou hast not laboured, neither madest it grow; which came up in a night, and perished in a night:

And should not I spare Nineveh, that great city, wherein are more than sixscore thousand persons that cannot discern between their right hand and their left hand; and also much cattle?

Jonah 4:5-11

God said (paraphrased), "Jonah, you have had concern and respect for that gourd that was over your head because a worm came and destroyed it. Now Jonah, can't I have that same concern for a city of more than 170,000 people who don't know their right hand from their left spiritually?"

God was after the people! He was after the city of Nineveh, the harvest of 170,000 souls. How many cities do you suppose there are on the face of this earth where God can't get a man or a people to feel the same way about the city as He does?

God knew Jonah was the man for the job in Nineveh, and He was willing to go to great lengths to deal with Jonah's pride. Finally Jonah had to come to the same conclusion John the Baptist did, that he had to decrease so that Jesus could increase. (John 3:30.) He had an amazing level of faith. It takes more faith to decrease so Jesus can increase than it does for you to increase.

I know people say it's brash and bold when Caldwell says God is going to deliver the city into his hands for the preaching of the gospel. But I didn't say that to myself. I would not have been smart enough to think of that! Why does God do these things? Because He loves people. He wants people to be saved, healed, and delivered.

We have to keep our priorities in the right order. God didn't call us just to build a church. He called us to build a church to reach a city. Every petition I bring before Him has to do with that calling. He called me to preach to my city, and when I get to heaven and He gives me my rewards, I'm just going to turn around and pass them on back to everybody who labored with me.

God has raised up a whole generation of faith people to go forth with the Word of God in all boldness and reach their cities for God. What we learn from Jonah is not to run from that calling and to care more for the people of our city than ourselves and our reputation. If we will just do what God tells us to do the way He tells us to do it, love the people and hate the sin, and trust Him to do the rest — look out devil and look out world!

Chapter 11
Partnershipping With Your City

It would be time-consuming to share all the details of how we have carried out God's call on our lives to reach our city, but I feel it is imperative to give you some of our specific methods and purposes, and especially to share the fruit of our labors with you. Fruit that remains is important. Without the fruit, there is no evidence that your efforts are working!

Habakkuk said that at the end, the vision will speak. (Habakkuk 2:3.) We can say that the vision is speaking and people are listening in Little Rock. Our city is changing and there is a God-consciousness here.

Change is part of living. It is not an option. If you are going to reach your city, state, nation, and world, you must be willing to change in your methods to reach people. While God and His Word do not change, His methods do.

To be successful in your vision you must be willing to follow the Holy Spirit's leading. We have used many different tools and methods to reach our city. Furthermore, your city may be entirely different from our city. What works for me may not work for you, and vice versa.

When God told Jonah to go to Nineveh, He simply told him to preach an eight-word sermon. Then the governor picked up his message and had it published throughout city. The result of following God's instruction was total repentance.

A minister friend of mine shared with me how God told him to go preach on Bourbon Street during Mardi Gras.

When he got there and stood up to preach, people ignored him. He quietly retreated to the alley and said, "God, I know you told me to come here. What's the matter? Nothing is happening."

God said to him, "You have to get their attention first. Call them what they are and you will have a crowd."

He went back to the street corner and hollered, "All you pimps, prostitutes, drunkards, drug addicts, and homosexuals, listen to me...." All of a sudden, he had a crowd. He had to change his method. He was preaching to street people. After you get their attention, then you give people the Word.

Creating a God-Consciousness

God said He would *deliver the city into our hands for the preaching of the gospel.* He didn't say everyone in the city would be saved, nor did He say they would all come to our church. He just said He would give us the opportunity to preach the gospel to our city — which He has.

Our first obedience to God was to begin our church. Everything proceeds from the local church. God will bring many people to the church who have key roles to play in bringing the gospel to your city. You don't have to have all the ideas yourself. You just have to know which ideas are from God.

Our congregation has always understood our vision and assignment from God. They know it was not my vision — it was God's vision. I am not the reason for the church, I am a gift to the church.

A young man came to me with something he believed was from God. This young man had designed a billboard and bumper sticker campaign to run in our city. The billboards were red, white, and blue and simply said in large letters, "Jesus is Lord over Little Rock."

We bought billboards around the city and had bumper stickers to match. We also gave the bumper stickers to other churches to give to their congregations. Soon, there were cars everywhere proclaiming, "Jesus is Lord over Little Rock."

In time other churches in other cities wanted to know if they could have bumper stickers proclaiming Jesus is Lord over their city. As a result, we began to supply them for other cities.

Television

In the mid-eighties, we began a weekly one-hour broadcast of our church service on the local CBS affiliate station at 6:00 a.m. on Sunday morning. Then we took our television cameras into the shopping malls during Easter and Christmas and asked people, "What do you think Easter is?" and "What do you think Christmas is about?" We also asked them what they thought about our billboards proclaiming, "Jesus is Lord over Little Rock."

We were pleasantly surprised by their answers. Most people knew what Christmas and Easter were about, and they liked our signs. What were we doing? We were creating a God-consciousness in our city and putting it on television for everyone to see. We were reminding our city who Jesus is, and we were taking Jesus out of the church building and holding Him up in the city. Jesus said, "If I be lifted up, I will draw all men unto Me."

You can't wait for people to come to your church, you have to go to them.

In 1988, we built the first full-power Christian television station for Pine Bluff and Little Rock in the history of our state. The second full-power station in our network was built and on the air in Hot Springs in 1995. *The Victory Television Network,* consisting of full-power Christian stations, is a reality in Arkansas and continues to add stations.

As we obeyed the Holy Spirit's specific instructions, we began to see "how" God was going to "deliver the city into our hands for the preaching of the gospel." Television reaches into people's homes, hotel rooms, hospitals, bars, and everywhere people are found.

We cover six thousand square miles with one station alone, not to mention all the cable systems we are on. Our ability to reach our city increased tremendously when we went on television.

I realize not everyone can own television stations or even go on television. Everyone is not called to do that, but we were. That was part of our assignment.

Television has become the dominant medium in our culture. We have more television sets in America than we do people. Television has affected how people respond to things. In fact, the entertainment industry has tried to become the value system of our culture, and we must never allow that to happen. Our churches must set the standard for morality and right and wrong in America.

What you get on television are "stories," and the people who watch a lot of television are story people. That's good news for us, because Jesus was the best storyteller Who ever lived! Television allows us to tell the gospel story, and has also caused us to look again at the parables of Jesus as a method of communication.

Years ago we said, "Just preach the Word of God and the people will come." While that's still true, what has changed is "how" we preach the Word. We do it with drama, with demonstrations, and with stories. We put it on different levels to reach different groups of people.

When I asked the Lord why this was true, He reminded me that Jesus taught in parables and that man's imagination is structured to see and think in pictures. That's why men wrote using pictures before they wrote using an alphabet to structure sentences. When post-Adamite civilizations recorded the story of Adam and Eve, they wrote in pictures, not words.

This is the structure of faith. Faith is the substance and evidence of things hoped for and things not "seen" yet. (Hebrews 11:1.) You have to *see* what you desire before you can possess it. Therefore, television is a creative tool to preach the gospel and teach people God's Word.

Ministering to the City

Next, we began to go into the projects in our city and minister to the residents. One day each month we have tent crusades for adults, youth, and children all at the same time. Teams of workers from our Evangelism Department, Youth Department, and Children's Department minister during these monthly crusades.

Food is given out and people are blessed by our love and concern. Then, each Monday evening, we go back into those projects and have Bible Studies for the residents. Five different teams minister the Word to these residents in their homes each week. On Sundays we send our bus to bring those who want to come to church.

Victims of Crime

The Victims of Crime Outreach program is another ministry to our city. This program was the heart's desire of our Mayor. He asked if we would help him reach out to families of victims of crime. In the event of a death, Victims of Crime Outreach provides four different teams to go and visit with the victim's families to provide prayer, counseling, financial assistance, and to meet other needs. The mayor tries to go on each visit, along with a minister, social worker, and city official. We are one of several churches serving in this ministry to our city.

A Church for Gangs

When HBO ran a rather hyped-up story on "gang banging" in Little Rock, a concerned ministry to gangs in California came to Little Rock and spied out the land to see if God was speaking to them to start a church for gang members.

Victory Outreach, comprised of ex-gang members, came to Little Rock and began with two great drama performances at our largest coliseum. Thousands attended to see the dramatization of gang life in the inner city. Hundreds responded to the altar call, and Victory Outreach Church for gangs was born in Little Rock.

Victory Outreach leaders said they had never been so warmly received and supported like they were in Little Rock. They have churches in hundreds of US cities. Now we are partnershipping with other churches in our city to provide Victory Outreach with a new home for their pastor. Also, we all agreed to help underwrite this ministry together for a year to get them started. That's ministering to your city!

A Jail Church

When our Agape School of World Evangelism Prison Ministry went to the Faulkner County Jail and held a revival meeting, quite a few inmates were saved. Out of that meeting, an Agape Church began in the jail. Their pastor and all the leadership are inmates.

They are provided a room in which to meet, and we helped with a sound system. They have church three times a week and give tithes and offerings, which are used to help other inmates.

I received a letter from the Sheriff in which he said, "What more could you ask for than an inmate population who are born again?" Praise God! That's ministering to your city!

106

Individual Ministries

A businessman in our church worked in the financial arena of investment banking. He wrote a book about managing your money, and began a small group study course on "Financial Freedom." The county allowed him to teach this course to the inmates at the Pulaski County Detention Center. After they completed the course, they graduated, and the ceremony was carried on the local news channel as, "Helping inmates learn to stay out of jail and become self-sufficient."

This businessman and his partners have also authored courses and provided business opportunities for small contractors to learn how to compete for large construction jobs in their city.

God told us we would be a "spiritual production center" and produce life throughout our city, state, nation, and world. God spoke the vision to me in the beginning, but again, I don't have to have all the ideas myself. I just need to know which ideas are of God. Then I encourage people to come forth and do what God has called them to do.

We simply provide a place of nourishment and incubation for people to be productive. As you can see through these testimonies, God will open doors for you to work with other churches and governmental offices in your city. I am not able to tell you all the areas of ministry God has given us. They are too many to include in this book.

Our newly appointed Chief of the Arkansas State Police is a born-again, Spirit-filled believer who teaches the Word. The first black man to be appointed as United States Marshall to Eastern Arkansas is a member of our church and a born-again, Spirit-filled man.

Our Governor is a former pastor and an evangelical who was formerly President of the Southern Baptist

Convention in Arkansas. Now, you tell me God isn't working in our city!

We have Bible Schools in some of our state prisons, even one on death row. They march in wearing leg irons to go to Bible class. Hallelujah! God is "delivering the city into our hands for the preaching of the gospel!"

Faith Christian High School

Our most recent endeavor is one I am very excited about. I think Faith Christian High School is the first of its kind in our city and state.

Four pastors and churches came together, along with concerned businessmen and educators, to form a Spirit-filled Junior High and High School for all students, especially those who are of low-income families.

We managed to get donations and grants from the business community to assist those who could not afford tuition. Together, we supplied the initial start-up costs. We all sent faculty members from our churches, and we all feed students into the school from our elementary schools.

We believe Faith Christian High School could be a model for the state and nation. This is just another way to reach your city for God.

A Final Word

God is a God of cities. I believe He has proved that to me and to our church as we have labored almost two decades now to carry out the word He gave to me, "I will deliver the city into your hands for the preaching of the gospel."

We had a sign in our office that says, "The reason some people let opportunity pass them by is because opportunity often comes disguised as hard work." Anyone in our church who has been a part of reaching our city will tell you it is hard work. But they will also tell you that the rewards go far beyond what they had ever imagined.

I truly believe that the key to the success we have seen in Little Rock is very simple. In fact, it is found in our church's name: Agape Church. As we started to obey God's specific instructions, He gave us a supernatural, unconditional love for the people of our city.

When we have God's love for the people operating in us, then we have the right motivation and unlimited strength and courage to preach the gospel to them and bless them, whether they accept Jesus and our message or not.

It has always bothered me when churches rail against their city with a militant spirit and try to "take" their city. These churches almost always fail, because they did not love the people unconditionally. Instead of believing God for lives to be transformed by His Spirit, they simply wanted to conquer and control their city.

However, love never fails. When you reach out to the people of your city with the unconditional love of Jesus Christ, the Holy Spirit is given full power to draw them to Him. There is nothing more satisfying and fulfilling than seeing a life touched and changed by Jesus Christ — and that is what this last great harvest is all about!

About the Author

Happy Caldwell is the Founder and Pastor of Agape Church, a strong, Spirit-filled body of believers in Little Rock, Arkansas. He is Founder and President of The Victory Television Network, which operates two full-power Christian television stations in Little Rock and Hot Springs, Arkansas. He is also President of the International Convention of Faith Ministries (ICFM) located in Little Rock, Arkansas.

Happy has an anointed way of presenting the Word of God in profound simplicity, making the character of God a revelation to those who hear. In 1979, God spoke to him to build a spiritual production center which would deliver the gospel throughout Little Rock, Arkansas, the United States, and the world. The Spirit of God has instructed him in the principles of taking a city for Jesus Christ. Through this revelation and a daily television program, "Arkansas Alive" (via The Victory Television Network), the city of Little Rock is being changed into a "city of light."

Traveling worldwide, Happy has imparted the same powerful revelation into the body of Christ, instructing them how to take their cities for God. Through his firm manner and deep sensitivity to the Spirit of God, the lost are saved, the sick are healed, the oppressed are delivered, and untold thousands are blessed.

Happy has recorded several record albums and is known for his heartfelt worship to God. He has also authored several books.

For a brochure of books and tapes
by Happy Caldwell, write:

Pastor Happy Caldwell
Agape Church
P. O. Box 22007
Little Rock, AR 72221-2007

The Harrison House Vision

Proclaiming the truth and power
Of the Gospel of Jesus Christ
With excellence;

Challenging Christians to
Live victoriously,
Grow spiritually,
Know God intimately.

HARRISON HOUSE
Tulsa, Oklahoma